Furniture
of the
Depression Era

Furniture and Accessories
of the
1920s, 1930s and 1940s

Robert W. and Harriett Swedberg

Furniture
of the
Depression Era

Furniture and Accessories
of the
1920s, 1930s and 1940s

Robert W. and Harriett Swedberg

COLLECTOR BOOKS
A Division of Schroeder Publishing Co., Inc.

The current values in this book should be used only as a guide. They are
not intended to set prices, which vary from one section of the country to
another. Auction prices as well as dealer prices vary greatly and are
affected by condition as well as demand. Neither the Author nor the
Publisher assumes responsibility for any losses that might be incurred as
a result of consulting this guide.

Additional copies of this book may be ordered from:

Collector Books
P.O. Box 3009
Paducah, KY 42002-3009

@ $19.95. Add $2.00 for postage and handling.

Printed by IMAGE GRAPHICS, INC., Paducah, Kentucky

Acknowledgements

The authors wish to express their sincere appreciation to the following collectors and dealers who so unselfishly gave of their time to assist in obtaining photographs and prices for this book. We extend a thanks, too, to those countless individuals who did not wish to be named. Without the help of these people this book would not have been possible.

Antiques at the Sign of the Gaslight, Richard Oxenrider, Pierceton, IN.

The Antique Shoppe, Dick & Janaan Harms, Rochelle, IL.

The Antique Showroom, Doug Brown, Waterloo, IA.

The Art Deco and Vintage Clothing Show, Indianapolis, IN.

A's House of Stuff 'N Things, Anna & Bob Figg, Buffalo, IA.

Attic Treasures, Donna Ramirez, Moline, IL.

Auld Lang Syne Antiques, Kathy Spear, Raymond, IA.

B & D Antiques, Bob & Darlene Parker, Chariton, IA.

Banowetz Antiques, Virl & Cathy, Maquoketa, IA.

Bob's Trading Post, Bob & Mary Ritter, Wilmington, IL.

Joan & Max Boynton, Galesburg, IL.

Broadway Antique Mall, Sam & Phyllis Sauley, Madison, IN.

Buggy Wheel Antiques, Bill & Gwen Carter, Warsaw, IN.

Carter Building, Ed Armbrust, Fred Maxheimer & Rick Ackerman, Mahomet, IL.

Barry Cholak & Rod Ewing, Cincinnati, OH.

Coachman Antique Mall, Kathie & John Small, La Porte, IN.

Colonial Antiques, Al & Gladys Wilkinson, Frederick, MD.

Country Corners, Ltd., Jerry & Jeanne Plagge, Latimer, IA.

The Country Workshop, A Mini Mall, Galesburg, IL.

Violet & John Cremer, Galesburg, IL.

Crossroads Antique Mall, Jane Parsons, Seymour, IN.

The Curiosity Shop, Bob & Joan Plew, Pierceton, IN.

Delzell's Country Antiques, Kirk & Sue Delzell, Morning Sun, IA.

Dover Pond Antiques, Sally Johnson & Dolores Reid, Waterford, WI.

Glenn & Mary Ann Estes, Kewanee, IL.

Four Flags Antique Mall, Jeannie Gilbert, Marie Majerek & Debbie Toman, Niles, MI.

4 Season Antiques, Jerry Silvers & Rick Spees, Birmingham, IA.

The Furniture House, Wynn & Pat Scott, Bradford, IL.

Martha Gibson.

Harlan & Marlene Glandorf, Hiawatha, IA.

Grand River Merchants of Williamston, Williamston, MI.

Mr. & Mrs. Robert Hingstrum.

Bertha & Wayne Hoffman.

Housman's Antiques, Jan & Dick, Pleasant Valley, IA.

J & J Antiques and Used Furniture, Hanover, IN.

Nancy Jones, Indianapolis, IN.

The Junque Shop, Al Horsley, Bucyrus, OH.

Kirkham's Korner Antiques, Dolores & Daniel, Pierceton, IN.

Lawton Antique Mall, Ruby & Bill Farrow, Don Hover, Dick & Sadie Schuessler, Lawton, MI.

The Louisville Antique Mall, Harold L., Chuck & Don Sego, Louisville, KY.

Nancy Lowery, Coal Valley, IL.

Main Street Antique Mall, Betty Applegate, Jeanne Newton & Rita Mullins, New Albany, IN.

Main Street Antiques, Mahomet, IL.

Memory Lane Antiques, Joan Dautch, Williamsville, NY.

Mr. & Mrs. Joe Moore.

Clara & Raymond Muhleman.

Old Time Sake Antiques, Jerry Liszewski, Amherst, WI.

Pauline Olson.

The Parson's House, Marilyn Johnson, Port Byron, IL.

Pat's Stripping, Pat Danen, Mahomet, IL.

Peddler Antique Mall, Dick & Pat Bouwkamp, Monticello, IN.

Plainfield Avenue Antique Mall, Larry & Gloria Pratt, Grand Rapids, MI.

The Red Hens, Jackie Irvine & Pat Pinnell, Paris, IL.

River Bend Antiques and Gifts, Ronald Bellomy, Arlene Bogaert & Laura Heath, Davenport, IA.

Rug Beater Antiques, Evelyn Gibson & Richard L. Schnick, Galesburg, IL.

School House Antiques, Kay Guzzards, Holcomb, IL.

Denny & Ann Schwartz.

Helen Shaffer.

The Sign of the Pineapple, Judy Wilkinson, Williamston, MI.

Silvers' House of Antiques, Barb & Jerry, Fairfield, IA.

Stephanie's Antiques, Stephanie Baldwin, Indianapolis, IN.

Trash Can Annie Clothes of the Past, Davenport, IA.

Twentieth Century Design, Benjamin Gold & Michael Kravitz, Philadelphia, PA.

Upper Level Antiques, James W. Romine, Jr. & Thomas E. Bishel, Galesburg, IL.

Village Bookstore, Robin McNish & Dee Barnet, Mahomet, IL.

Mrs. Virlea G. Voges.

Wanna Buy a Duck, David & Carroll Swope, Canton, OH.

The Watsons, Adam, Cody, Karen & Terry.

Webb's Antique Mall, Verlon Webb, Centerville, IN.

Mrs. John Yolton.

Contents

Chapter One

Introduction
Pricing, Dating and Identification of Veneers

The prices of the furniture and accessories found in this book have been established by the dealers and collectors who own them. We, the authors, have used this "price tag" policy in our other furniture price guides. The values listed, however, are intended as guides only, and neither the authors nor the publisher assumes responsibility for any losses that may be incurred as a result of using this book.

As yet, furniture and accessories of the 1920s, 1930s and 1940s are not for sale in large quantities in antiques shops throughout the country. Since there is no current guide, the pricing of objects from this time period is subjective and wide variances are apparent. A 1920 walnut veneered buffet, for example, was priced at $125.00 in one area and a similarly constructed piece was tagged at $450.00 in another locale.

Many factors can influence value assessments. One is the price a dealer paid for an article. Another is the condition of the piece and how much repair or refinishing is required to put it into usable shape. Also, the fanciness of the article - the extent of veneering, hand painting or applied carvings or decorations - influence the sales tag. Nostalgia often causes individuals to treasure a family piece and price it beyond its actual worth. Furniture from this time period is not readily seen for sale in all areas of the country, but there are locales where it is beginning to appear in shops. Because this furniture is not considered old enough, it is not accepted everywhere.

Finding appropriate pieces of furniture and accessories to photograph required thousands of miles of travel through a dozen states. Many shops visited had no examples while others had only a few. Antique shows, in general, were devoid of this era furniture. Our greatest success occurred in the large malls where antiques and collectibles were featured.

Because much of the furniture manufactured during the 1920s, 1930s and 1940s copied 18th and 19th century period styles or modified them, confusion sometimes exists among dealers as to the real age of a piece. If you become aware of the different woods used and the changes in construction methods employed during these time periods, you can avoid this uncertainty.

Two examples are given to illustrate this point. A walnut veneered china cabinet of the Jacobean type was found in one shop priced at $1,800.00. This would have been a fair market price if the piece had been from the 17th century when this style was prevalent, but it was a copy made during the 1920s. Its value, according to others we have seen, should have been in the $250.00 to $300.00 range. The dealer was not attempting to deceive the public. He was simply uninformed as to the differences that exist between a 17th century Jacobean china cabinet and one made in the 1920s.

At a midwestern antiques show, we saw a game table with a ribbon-striped mahogany veneered top and a mahogany stained hardwood base. Because this type of mahogany was used, we were able to determine that this table was a 1920 copy of an earlier piece. Through a lack of understanding of the construction and wood characteristics, the dealer mistakenly claimed it was a circa 1840 game table.

We have dated each article pictured in this book. Where an exact year is mentioned, such as 1925, we have evidence from the owner that this was when it was originally purchased. Other dates - early, middle or late 1920s, 1930s, 1940s - are based on examples seen in the catalogues we examined. Thirty three Chittendon-Eastman catalogues, representing 120 furniture makers, and catalogues from Sears, Montgomery Ward, Baker Furniture Company, Kittinger Company, Inc. and Imperial Furniture were consulted for this purpose.

Identifying the veneers used on the furniture pictured in this book has been difficult.

The United States Department of Agriculture's forest service division supports this contention when it says, "No two pieces of wood show the same figure. In some hardwoods the figure is often made more prominent by the use of dark, or occasionally, light colored fillers. The identification of woods is not a simple matter because there are many kinds and each kind varies more or less in appearance and properties within itself. For example, some mahogany lumber is light colored and other lumber of the same species is dark colored. Furthermore, there are often puzzling superficial resemblances between unrelated species; as, for example between birch and maple and between cherry and mahogany. Lumbermen, manufacturers and dealers in furniture usually recognize the more common woods by general appearance but this method is only fairly accurate for a limited number of woods."

Furniture manufacturers of this period further complicated wood identification by bleaching, staining and dyeing the hardwoods and veneers they used.

The prestigious Victoria and Albert Museum in London, that we recently visited, has a magnificient display of period furniture that features exotic inlays, marquetry and varied veneer patterns. The curators there, too, recognize the extreme difficulty in naming woods and as a consequence, very few specific veneers are identified. Instead, general descriptions such as these are used: "Inlay of various woods. Marquetry decorations. Veneered and inlaid with various woods."

It would have been easier for us to follow a similar procedure, but we felt that this approach would not have satisfied the readers. In order to name the veneers as accurately as possible, we studied extensively in books dealing with veneers and examined scores of actual veneer samples. Then through the examination of the furniture catalogues, we became aware of the veneers that were used during the 1920s, 1930s and 1940s because they were identified by the photographs in the catalogues. Even though we were as exacting as possible, we are aware that there may be some errors in identification.

We know by research for example, that an article that is listed as late 1930s was also produced at an earlier or later date because furniture styles last a long time. Pictures seen in catalogues show this to be true. The Governor Winthrop secretaries that have been made continuously from the 1920s through the 1940s exemplify this. One example shown in this book is listed as 1927 because, according to the owner's mother, this was the year in which it was purchased.

An overall observation after completing this project is that the 1920s and 1930s furniture and accessories are beginning to find their way into shops around the country. Some are accepted at antique shows. A 1930 curio cabinet, pictured in this book, was photographed at a midwestern show in the fall of 1985. In contrast, however, the 1940s furniture is still remaining in private homes.

Dealers have shared observations with us as to what is currently marketable. China cabinets, they say, sell well, but the long buffets are not as quick to move because they take up more space. A server is smaller and easier for a home to accommodate and as a consequence outsells the buffets. These shop owners concluded that sets consisting of a china cabinet, table and six chairs have greater general appeal than the ten-piece sets that include both a buffet and server.

In bedroom furniture, dressing tables and benches are popular and many women prefer the type with a level top that allows them easy access to both their cosmetics and the mirror as they sit in comfort to apply their make-up. Vanities with drop centers are not so handy. Preference is shown for the dressing table with three mirrors since the two side ones can be adjusted to enable the user to see her face, profile and the back of her hair. Small occasional tables, even though modestly priced, do not sell well unless, of course, they have fancy carvings and attractive veneers.

These observations should clarify the pricing, dating and veneer naming procedures used in this book.

Examples of Catalogue Listings of Veneers
Used on Furniture

Catalogue Year	Catalogue Listing
1923	Walnut veneered tops and ends with figured walnut veneered fronts.
1924	Carefully matched genuine walnut veneered tops, fronts and ends.
1925	Genuine figured walnut veneered tops and fronts with plain walnut ends and burl walnut overlays.
1926	Selected genuine walnut veneered tops and ends with matched butt walnut veneer on two lower drawers, upright mottled veneer on two small drawers and blistered maple decorations on panels and mirror supports.
1926	Genuine walnut veneered tops and ends with matched butt walnut veneer on fronts and blistered maple decorations, gilded carving, green polychrome shading and hand-painted floral decorations.
1927	Selected five ply genuine walnut veneer on tops and ends with matched butt walnut veneers and diamond figured mahogany veneers on drawer fronts.
1928	Walnut veneered tops and ends with crotch walnut and figured walnut veneered fronts and overlays of African walnut veneer.
1929	Oriental walnut veneers on tops, ends and fronts with reversed diamond-matched zebrawood and madrone overlays on fronts.
1929	East Indian rosewood veneered tops, ends and fronts with overlays of Macassar ebony and Carpathian elm.
1931	Walnut veneered tops, ends and fronts with matched butt walnut veneered fronts and decorations of basket weave zebrano wood veneer and quilted maple overlays.
1931	Mahogany veneered tops and ends with crotch mahogany veneered fronts trimmed with satinwood and burl redwood veneer.
1932	Genuine satinwood veneered tops and ends with diamond-matched satinwood veneered fronts decorated with maple burl, aspen crotch and tulipwood veneers.
1932	Genuine walnut veneered top, ends and front with figured butt walnut, V-matched satinwood panels and quilted poplar veneered overlays.
1934	Blistered maple veneered tops and ends with burl Acacia veneered fronts.
1934	Satinwood veneered tops, end and fronts with koa veneered panels and tulipwood veneered banding.
1935	Gumwood base with stenciled decorations and fiddleback maple veneerite decorations.
1935	East India satinwood veneered tops, ends and fronts with crotch aspen veneer, floral decorations and genuine inlay marquetry on drawer fronts.
1936	Diamond-matched tigerwood veneered fronts flanked by butt walnut veneer.
1937	Sliced walnut veneered tops and ends with marowood and diamond-matched walnut veneered fronts.
1938	Genuine Mexican, mountain grown striped colobra (kelobra) tops and ends with colobra crotch veneered drawer fronts in conjunction with V-matched Orientalwood veneers.
1939	Sliced walnut veneered tops and ends, butt walnut veneered fronts with claro wood crotch veneer on front of top drawers.
1943	Dull lacquered walnut or bleached mahogany finish with quarter striped walnut and fiddleback mahogany veneered tops, ends and fronts.
1949	Combination walnut and gum with walnut veneered tops and ends, mahogany veneered panels and V-matched mahogany center panels.

Chapter Two

Characteristics of Household Furnishings
of the 1920s, 1930s and 1940s

Changes buffeted the United States in the 1920s, manifesting themselves in many ways. Interior decoration in homes did not escape its onslaught. Furniture styles were influenced by historical and technical developments. An overall view of events and inventions helps show why and how new household furnishings developed.

This nation entered World War I in 1917, and when it ended in 1918, turmoil ran rampant. When the men marched off to war, many women worked in factories. They gained greater independence and sought to keep it. Females demanded the right to vote and in August, 1920, the Nineteenth Amendment to the Federal Constitution made this possible. Many women chopped off both their floor length skirts and their long hair. Unconventional bold females, called Flappers, danced the fast-paced Charleston, wore low-waisted, knee-length dresses, rolled their stockings and covered their bobbed hair with snug, cloche (bell-shaped) hats. The syncopated beat of jazz throbbed at night spots. With their status different, it was natural that women wanted their homes updated to express their new freedom. Many coveted modern furniture.

Men, too, felt the turbulance. These World War I veterans had seen novel sights and had had new experiences. "How can you keep them down on the farm after they've seen 'Paree'" was a popular song with a note of truth in it. Population wise, rural Americans outnumbered urban dwellers until 1920 when the U.S. census indicated half of the people resided in cities. This urban trend continued because, in that year alone, some 200,000 tractors did the chores faster than horses guided by men and a smaller labor force was required.

In many cases, the tempo of life quickened, but, naturally, not every community was changed with the onset of the Roaring Twenties. Some localities retained their usual pattern undisturbed by a new morality standard that overlooked the onslaught of political scandals, the growth of organized crime, and the emergence of a freer sex code.

Cellarette with walnut veneer outside and mahogany veneer inside, 23" wide, 14" deep, 44" high, late 1930s. This liquor cabinet held necessities for preparing alcoholic beverages. It appeared in some homes after liquor was legalized in 1933.

In 1920, the Eighteenth Amendment, which forbade the manufacture, transportation and sale of alcoholic beverages, went into effect. Sociologists contended that this promoted organized crime since various gangs sought to control bootleg whiskey and their activities became octupus-like as they ensnared other businesses as well. When Amendment Twenty One repealed the Eighteenth in 1933, new furniture forms including cocktail tables, cellarettes, liquor and hospitality cabinets evolved to accommodate the now available liquor.

Bow end bed with bird's-eye maple panels and selected hardwood frame, 56″ wide, 47″ high at headboard, 32″ high at footboard, 1920s. Low head and foot boards replaced the tall, oversized beds of the late 1800s. Bow end beds with six feet were stylish.

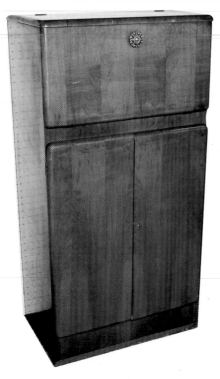

Closed view of cellarette.

Industrially, the nation felt an upheaval and its effect on the home was profound. Many technological advancements influenced the production of furniture. Both a router to cut out recesses and the automatic wood lathe to shape wood were introduced in the early 1900s. A multiple carver with horizontal carving heads that carved 24 or more identical parts for furniture simultaneously appeared in the 1920s. A spray gun replaced the brush for applying finish and reduced the amount of hand labor formerly required for this task.

In 1908, Henry Ford decided that volume sales, not high mark-ups, would increase profits in the automobile field. From 1920 to 1921 his company sold 1,250,000 autos. By 1936 there were a total of 26,167,000 cars and trucks in the United States, traveling along 3,040,000 miles of highway of which one million were paved. Suburbs grew as easy transportation allowed workers to move out of the city and commute to their jobs. Suburbanites desired updated home decorations for their new life styles and furniture manufacturers were eager to please them.

Airplanes flew and children who heard their drone rushed out to watch them. Although an official airmail flight was made in 1911, it was not until 1918 that the first regular United States airmail service was established to unite New York City, Philadelphia and Washington, D.C. After a test transcontinental flight proved successful in 1923, coast-to-coast airmail service began operating in 1924. America was interested in speed and various designers tried to depict this intangible concept in their artistic efforts. Streamlined became a designer term. Tubular steel and other metal furniture appeared. Sleek greyhounds, automobiles and airplanes were depicted on home accessory items to convey the idea of rapid motion.

Communication systems developed. The telephone that seemed to be a toy when it was invented in 1876 became, in sixty years, a boon to business and to homes. In 1936, 17,000,000 were in use in the United States and homes found special tables and chairs which served as a place to put telephones and to seat their users.

America's first broadcasting stations brought news, comedy, music, drama and religion into over fifty million homes. Instructions on child care, automobile repair and health were given over the air ways. Fancy cabinets originated to hold radios and homemakers sought those with eye appeal. The first President to appear on television was Franklin D. Roosevelt in 1939 and seven years later the postwar sale of TV sets began. These required cabinets also.

Other entertainment evolved. When the original nickelodeon opened in 1905, patrons paid five cents to view a twenty minute silent screen program as a pianist provided appropriate background mood music. Hollywood, California, became the movie capital of the world. In 1927 Warner Brothers produced "The Jazz Singer," the premier feature-length film with spoken dialogue. Afterwards talkies gradually replaced the silent screen and Hollywood stars influenced fashions. Perhaps that is why vanities and benches (dressing tables) soon became focal points in bedrooms and some were actually called Hollywood vanities.

Victor radio with solid walnut case, plain-cut walnut veneer panels and painted decorations, 34" wide, 21" deep, 57" high, 1929. This radio has a Jacobean cabinet after an English style popular from about 1603 to 1649. Furniture of that period was large, square or rectangular and the wood was lavishly carved in low relief.

The incandescent bulb was inserted in cabinets, vanities and chests in the late 1920s as electricity both lighted the home and lightened the work load with the development of appliances. Special tables were designed for lamps. The rapid acceptance of electricity is apparent in the following statistics. In 1889 electricity generated only two percent of the power needed by American industry, but by 1919 this figure rose to thirty-one percent.

Progress brought other changes as well. For example, in the 1920s, bathrooms and indoor plumbing were an accepted part of urban living. Commodes and washstands became outmoded. As late as the 1940s they were needed in rural areas where the outdoor privy still stood at the end of the backyard path.

Economically, most of the nation experienced a postwar prosperity. An old adage, "Neither a borrower nor a lender be," became passe as businesses coaxed possible patrons to buy on time. The theme, enjoy the merchandise as you make monthly payments, encouraged people to go into debt to buy household furnishings, farm machinery and automobiles.

Suddenly, prosperity vanished in 1929 as an economic depression hit much of the world. Now the frivolous twenties were replaced by the hard-time thirties. That's the depression era. Its impact was not phased out completely until World War II opened markets for military supplies in the early 1940s.

Another factor that influenced the furniture from the 1920s through the 1940s was the decline in the lumber supply. Early in the 1900s conservationists became concerned because the United States' virgin forests were being depleted, and they promoted measures to save the trees. In the main, manufacturers switched from constructing solid wooden furniture to using veneer, a thin layer of decorative wood glued over a strong core base.

Does the word "veneer" immediately conjure up a picture of cheap, inferior furniture? Do you consider veneering with its plywood construction a relatively new process? Do you think it is structurally weak? If you nodded yes, you are wrong. Exquisite furniture can be veneered. Thousands of years ago Egyptian craftsmen were creative. A mural retrieved from the tomb of a nobleman who lived centuries before Christ shows workmen preparing and applying veneer as they completed the lamination process. Beds, chairs, chests and tables retrieved from tombs of the pharoahs are veneered. This construction was used by the Romans also. The acceptance of veneering fluctuated greatly. It was stylish in the 1700s but declined thereafter only to be resurrected again in the 1920s.

An example of quality veneer work, a desk fit for King Louis XV (1710-1774) is on display at the Louvre Museum in Paris. Jean Henri Riesener spent nine years and over one million francs handcrafting it. The surface is covered with hand-sawed, meticulously matched veneers from the finest woods. Can't you imagine its designer disdainfully discarding all the pieces of veneer he found unworthy to be a part of his artistic creation? A 1929 Montgomery Ward & Company catalogue shows this famous "Bureau du Roi" and calls this desk "the most expensive piece of furniture in the world." At that time its value was $85,000.00.

This same Ward's catalogue pictures a salesman promoting veneers because the public, accustomed to solid furniture, needed to be educated. The caption reads, "Solid or Veneered, which is better? Veneered furniture is solid plus!"

The salesman explains, "Madame, this veneered top is much more beautiful, much more durable and offers a choice of grain not possible in solid wood. The forestry division of the U.S. Government has determined that veneered wood is 80 per cent stronger - nearly twice as strong - as solid wood of equal thickness!"

Parlor desk with plain-cut walnut veneer top and sides, butt walnut veneer on door and drawer panels, applied decorations and painted designs on top three drawers, 54″ wide, 20″ deep, 30″ high, 1930s.

The use of plywood propellers and fuselages for U.S. fighter planes flown in World War I is a forceful endorsement of the strength of veneers. Ply means a layer and five ply (five layers) is generally used for quality furniture. Plywood results when several thickness of veneer are glued together at right angles to the grain of the adjacent veneers. The alternation of grains helps counteract the wood's cross-grain weakness since it minimizes warping, contraction, expansion, reaction to weather conditions and splitting. This crisscross layering process is referred to as lamination. Strength plus beauty is a combination hard to beat.

Seng furniture facts (sic) published by The Seng Company, Chicago, states that in 1964 when this booklet came out, hardwood face veneers (the top layers) were usually one twenty-eighth of an inch thick. Crossband veneers (the first layer of veneer on each side of the core) were one-twentieth of an inch.

Inlay is a flush design formed by inserting woods, ivory, metal, shells and other materials of a contrasting color into tiny channels or grooves specifically cut in furniture parts to receive them. Ornamental patterns with flowers, borders and other decorative effects emerge. When an entire surface

Occasional table with 4-way V-matched padauk veneer, inlaid design, carved apron and French legs, 17″ square, 27″ high, early 1930s.

such as a table top, drawers or doors are covered with inlays spaced in a close pattern, the result is called marquetry or marquetry inlay. The design made of wood, ivory, metal or shell is frequently fitted into a pattern on a thin sheet of wood veneer and afterwards glued to the furniture.

Just as a wallpaper hanger matches the pattern of each consecutive strip, so veneer is matched to glamorize the appearance of furniture. The 1929 Montgomery Ward catalogue states, "With veneers selected for beauty of grain, it is possible to match the markings of a single beautiful log upon the broad surfaces of an entire suite. Each log cut into veneers is sent to one furniture factory where expert workmen match the veneers on the tops, fronts and ends of each suite. Without veneering, this beauty would be impossible."

Even the way the log is cut creates differences in the appearance of the grain. Plain-sawed results when an entire log is sliced in parallel lines lengthwise. In quarter-sawed lumber, the log is cut into four pieces and each is sliced into parallel boards across the annual rings so that the medullary rays or flakes are seen. This process cost more because additional handling is required and also some waste results. A rotary or peal cut veneer is unrolled from the log by rotating the log against a large knife. It's almost akin to paring an apple. Rotary veneer can be produced cheaply in large sheets and its growth ring figure is continuous. Sheets may be sliced, shaved or sawed in other ways also to create various effects. The person who decides how to cut a log is called a flitcher. An expert one can detect how the beauty of the resulting veneer can best be brought out and he saws the flitches (strips) accordingly.

Application differs also. Imagine a table top. The entire surface can be covered with one sheet of veneer or with two or more pieces. If different woods are combined, the result is more elaborate. Designs can be formed when small pieces of contrasting veneers are used to create an inlay pattern or a marquetry surface. At times router lines, incised channels, are used to separate the different veneers or solid woods on the fronts or tops of pieces. For example, the center of a drawer may be of mahogany veneer separated by router lines from walnut veneered ends.

Matched patterns are created in many ways. Since veneers are cut thin and stacked in consecutive order, the adjacent slices in each bundle or flitch carry similar grain and figure markings. In book matching, two consecutive sheets are removed from the pile, opened like a book and glued side-by-side to form a book matched pattern. When the sheets are matched lengthwise end to end rather than at the side, the result is called end matching. A four-way match is achieved by combining the two aforementioned patterns and using four adjacent sheets. Slide match indicates that the top sheet on the pile is slid into a side-by-side alignment with the sheet directly beneath it.

Lane cedar chest with V-matched Oriental walnut top and diamond-matched center panels flanked by butt walnut veneer panels, 47" wide, 18" deep, 23" high, middle 1930s. The rolled top was called "waterfall".

One special veneer known as burl is produced by cutting through the wart-like humps found on certain trees. In this country these abnormal or diseased growths occur more generally on walnut, maple and ash than on other species.

Impatient man couldn't wait for nature to create burls. French peasants of long ago discovered they could malform a tree by cutting off its top branches. This left the trunk intact so bushy new limbs grew. This produced a peculiar grain not unlike burl. The practice called "pollarding" became common. Natural conditions, such as gusts of winds that cause a tree to sway and the mineral content of the soil, influence how veneer looks. Each tree is a special creation and no two pieces of wood show an identical figure.

Crotch, a plume figure, is obtained from the portion of a tree where two large limbs unite. Butt veneer, also called stump, is cut from the stump of carefully selected trees where the roots branch off and the grain is irregular.

Bird's-eye veneer slightly resembles a bird's eye. Some say it occurs when buds grow too deep to break through the bark to the tree's surface. Other sources do not attempt to explain this natural phenomenon.

Occasional table with bird's-eye veneer top and bottom shelf and selected hardwood frame, 14" square, 28" high, 1920s.

The following four charts, "Veneers and Their Patterns Introduced in the Catalogues from 1920 through the 1940's," list the main kinds used. The accompanying illustrations show some of the figures and patterns inherent in veneers.

Veneers and Their Patterns
Introduced in the Catalogues from 1920 through 1928

Veneer	Pattern	Origin	Color
Gum	quarter-sawed	U.S.A.	redish-brown
Mahogany		Africa, West Indies, South America	light pink to reddish-brown and tannish brown
	burl		
	crotch		
	fiddleback		
	figured		
	mottled		
	plain-cut		
	rotary-cut		
	sliced		
	striped		
Madrone		Pacific coast from British Columbia to Mexico	reddish brown
Maple, hard		U.S.A.	cream to light reddish brown
	bird's-eye		
	blistered		
	figured		
Rosewood		South & Central America, India and Ceylon	dark brown - chocolate to violet with black streaks
Tulipwood		Brazil	light background with red & yellow streaks
Walnut		U.S.A., Canada	light gray brown to dark purplish-brown
	burl		
	butt (stump)		
	Circassian	Europe	tawny colored
	crotch	U.S.A., Canada	light gray brown to dark purplish-brown
	figured		
	plain-cut		
	rotary-cut		
	sliced		
	striped		
	stumpwood (butt)		

Veneer and Their Patterns Introduced in the Catalogues of 1929

Veneer	Pattern	Origin	Color
Avodire		West Africa	dull paper white to golden cream
Ebony, Macassar		East Indies	dark with light yellow or yellowish brown with light vertical markings
Elm		U.S.A.	light grayish-brown
	burl	France, England, Carpathian Mountains	brick-red to light tan
Elm, Carpathian		France, England, Carpathian Mountains	brick-red to light tan
English Sycamore (harewood or great maple)		England	natural white to yellow
Harewood (English sycamore or great maple)		England	natural white to yellow
Mahogany		Africa, West Indies, Central and South America	light pink to reddish brown and tannish brown
	beeswing		
	swirl		
Maple, hard		U.S.A.	cream to light reddish-brown
	burl		
	curly		
Oak	swirl	U.S.A.	light brown with a grayish tinge
Redwood	burl	U.S.A.	pink to deep red
Rosewood, East Indian		India, Ceylon	dark purple to ebony with streaks of red or yellow
	striped		
Satinwood		Ceylon, India, Puerto Rico, Honduras	varies from light bright yellow to dark brown
Zebrawood (zebrano)		Africa	straw with close straight brown stripes

Veneers and Their Patterns Introduced in the Catalogues of the 1930s

Veneer	Pattern	Origin	Color
Acacia	burl	U.S.A.	light to dark brown with black flecks
Amboyna (narra)		Borneo, East Indies	brown variegated yellow to red, changes to brown
Ash	quarter-sawed American	U.S.A., Canada	cream to light brown
Aspen	crotch figured	U.S.A.	pure white to whitish yellow
Birch	curly	U.S.A., Canada	cream or light brown tinged with red
Blackwood, Tasmanian		Australia, Tasmania	reddish brown to golden brown
Bubinga (African rosewood)		Africa	from pale to deep red
Cherry		U.S.A.	light reddish-brown
Claro (walnut)	crotch	U.S.A.	tannish brown with dark brown
Kelobra (colobra)		Mexico	brown with greenish cast
Koa		Hawaii	golden brown with black lines
Lacewood (Australian silky "oak")	diamond-matched	Australia	light pink with silvery sheen
Laurel (Acacia & myrtle burl	burl	U.S.A.	gray to brown with black lines
Maple, Australian (Queensland maple)	butt	Australia	light red
Maple, hard		U.S.A.	cream to light reddish-brown
	fiddleback quilted		
Narra (Amboyna burl)		East Indies, Philippines	brilliant browns to golden yellow
Olivewood, Italian	burl	Europe	yellowish brown
Orientalwood (Australian walnut)		Austrialia	pinkish gray to brown
	diamond-matched figured matched mottled V-matched		
Padauk (padouk)		Burma	yellow to golden red with brown
Paldao		Philippines	gray to reddish brown
Prima vera (primavera)		Central America	yellowish white to yellowish brown
Redwood	burl	U.S.A.	pink to deep red
Rosewood		Brazil	dark purple to dull reds and pinks but varies so no two logs are close in color
Satinwood	V-matched	Ceylon	pale gold
Tigerwood	diamond-matched	Africa	gray brown to gold with black streaks
Walnut	diamond-matched	U.S.A., Canada	light gray brown to dark purplish brown
	diamond-matched crotch figured butt four-way butt matched African	Africa	gray brown to gold with black streaks
	matched black stump	U.S.A., Canada	light gray brown to dark purplish brown
	matched butt matched stripe Oriental	Australia	pinkish gray to brown with dark stripes
	V-matched African	Africa	gray brown to gold with black streaks
	V-matched striped	U.S.A., Canada	light gray brown to dark purplish brown
Walnut (Claro)	crotch	U.S.A.	tannish brown with dark brown
Zebrawood (Zebrano)	basketweave	Africa	straw and dark brown with fine stripes
	V-matched		

Veneers and Their Patterns Introduced in the Catalogues of the 1940s

Veneer	Pattern	Origin	Color
Mahogany	herringbone matched	Africa, West Indies, Central & South America	light pink to reddish brown and tannish brown
Maple, Australian	matched burl	Australia	light red
New Guinea Wood		New Guinea, Philippines	gray to reddish brown
Orientalwood	V-matched beeswing V-matched striped	Australia	pinkish gray to brown
Paldao	diamond matched	Philippines	gray to reddish brown
Prima vera (primavera)	sliced	Central America	yellowish white to yellowish brown
Tigerwood	cross-banded	Africa	gray brown to gold with black streaks
Walnut	pin-striped	U.S.A., Canada	light gray brown to dark purplish brown
Zebrawood (Zebrano)	reverse diamond-sliced V-matched sliced diamond-matched	Africa	straw and dark brown with fine stripes

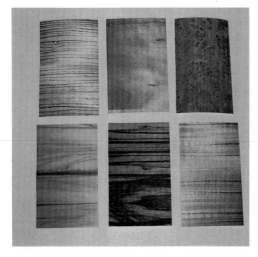

Veneers from upper left to bottom right: quartered zebrawood, Hawaiian koa, Carpathian elm burl, figured red gum, Macassar ebony and quartered paldao.

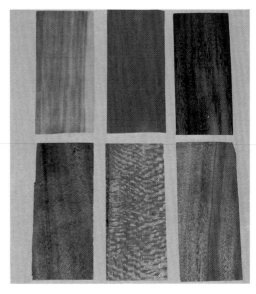

Veneers from upper left to bottom right: figured cherry, red gumwood, kelobra, koa, lacewood and plain mahogany.

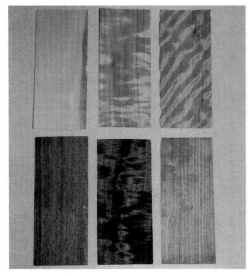

Veneers from upper left to bottom right: ash, aspen, mottled avodire, bubinga, African cherry, cherry.

Veneers from upper left to bottom right: South African rosewood, quartered elm, African rosewood, African mahogany, quartered narra and bird's-eye maple.

Veneers from upper left to bottom right: striped mahogany, myrtle burl, padauk, paldao, Indian rosewood, Honduras rosewood.

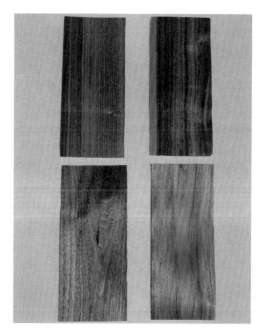

Veneers from upper left to bottom right: striped walnut, figured striped walnut, walnut and French walnut.

Borax was the name that was applied to the mass-produced, lower priced, poorly made, showy furniture of the 1920s and 1930s. Some say this moniker was derived from the premiums given with a cleaning compound containing borax. Others claim it is a foreign word corrupted. The illustrated chiffonier is an example. It is made of inexpensive hardwood, but with the aid of staining and artificial graining, it became a marketable product. The background caramel tone was permitted to dry before dark colored details were rolled or stamped on. This was a quicker process than cutting, matching and gluing veneers to a surface. The center of the second drawer was stained walnut. An imitation graining on the decorative panel was added and outlined by black router lines. Brown router lines separate a section of artificial graining from the walnut-stained space at the edge. When all the drawers were decorated in this manner, a showy chest was created. The plain drawer that shows was stripped with a water-wash paint remover, leaving the light colored hardwood base exposed. The construction of this chest fits the characteristics of cheap furniture found in the outline, entitled "Characteristics of Quality and Inexpensive Veneered Furniture" that follows later.

It is possible to finish this piece in a number of ways. Restore it with staining and graining. Stain it. Leave it light in tone with the surface protected with coats of varnish. Paint it or antique it.

A borax (cheap) chest of drawers with artificial graining stripped off one drawer to reveal the gumwood base. Note the router lines, applied decorations, and the burl walnut veneer panel on the bottom drawer, 34″ wide, 18″ deep, 52″ high, late 1920s.

Veneerite, a fake veneer printed on paper, is found on some inexpensive furniture. It peels off if paint remover is applied, and immediately all the pattern disappears. In contrast, genuine veneer found on more expensive furniture withstands a gentle, careful stripping and the application of new layers of varnish again reveals the beauty of its grain.

Characteristics of
Inexpensive and Quality Furniture

A. Inexpensive furniture
1. artificial graining
2. veneerite (fake veneer patterns printed on paper)
3. no dust dividers between drawers
4. no center guides for drawers
5. three-ply tops and sides
6. base wood (often gumwood) stained a walnut or mahogany
7. drawer sides and back made of a soft wood and bottoms made of cheap three-ply veneer
B. Quality furniture
1. selected figured hardwood veneers over a base wood
2. five-ply tops and sides
3. center guides for the drawers
4. dust dividers between drawers
5. three-ply drawer bottoms of oak or mahogany
6. drawer sides and backs of oak, sycamore or selected hardwoods
7. solid wood legs and posts of the same type as the face veneer
8. solid cases of cherry, mahogany, maple, oak, rosewood or walnut
C. Both inexpensive and quality furniture
1. applied wooden ornamentation
2. colored router lines separate two tone effects, different veneers and contrasting colors
3. painted touches

Some critics are prone to bypass much of the so-called Art Deco and classify examples mass manufactured for the installment trade as borax furniture. Do you realize that the term "Art Deco" is relatively new? The term was not listed in the thick annual distributors' catalogues researched by the authors that represented the output of over two hundred furniture factories from the 1920s, 1930s and 1940s.

The Seng Company of Chicago that pioneered Hollywood metal bed frames in 1937 did not include the name Art Deco in their 1964 instruction book for salesmen. It is not found in Joseph Aronson's *The Encyclopedia of Furniture* copyrighted in 1965, nor is it mentioned in *The Home Furnishing Arts* books of the 1930s perused at the Grand Rapids Public Library, or in microfilmed newspapers of the period.

Instead, the descriptive term was Art Moderne- "an extreme, modernistic French style launched at the Paris Exposition of 1925," Seng's book stated.

Katherine Morrison McClinton, a skilled researcher and an internationally recognized author, also attests to the fact that Art Moderne (or Art Décoratif) was the original name. Her qualifications include the fact that she attended the Exposition des Arts Décoratifs et Industriels Modernes in Paris in 1925. Her book *Art Deco, A Guide for Collectors*, copyrighted in 1972 asserts that a commemorative exhibition called "Les Anné'es '25" at the Musé'e des Arts Décoratifs was held in 1966 and developed renewed interest in this art form. Sometime after this event the term Art Deco emerged. Even a novice can guess that it represents a shortened version of *Arts Décoratifs*. Since Art Deco was not the term used in the Depression era, the name Art Moderne is used in this book.

An Art Moderne waterfall chiffonier (chest of drawers) with walnut veneer top, side and upper three drawers, V-matched Oriental wood on bottom drawer, zebrawood strips below top two drawers and celluloid and brass plated handles, 30" wide, 17" deep, 48" high, middle 1930s. Blue glass lamps and ceramic Madonna are from this period.

Advocates of this style realize that not all the furniture and accessories of the 1920s and 1930s was Art Moderne nor were all its chracteristics the same. It could be refined and delicate or of plastic and chrome. The latter was inexpensive and some consumers bought it eagerly. Others ignored it. Articles were both handmade and mass-produced. Paris was the fashion trend center as many people espoused a carefree, "let's enjoy luxury and pleasure" air. This exuberant spirit counteracted the privations imposed upon much of Europe during World War I. Slowly, Art Moderne invaded the United States, and its impetus was felt between 1925 and 1935.

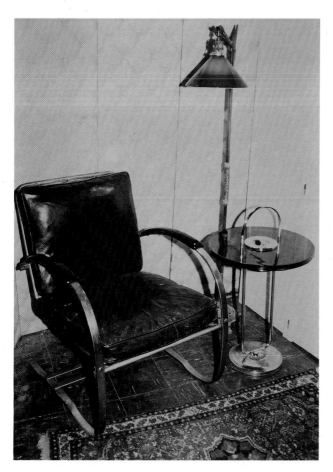

Chrome plated arm chair with covered cushions in artificial leather, 24" arm to arm, 31" high, middle 1930s. Metal furniture was in style until the late 1940s. The floor lamp with the green glass shade and the chrome ash tray with the black composition top are also from this period.

Prior to that, from about 1895 through 1910, Art Nouveau's exaggerated curves and asymmetrical forms were present. As Art Moderne styles began, media such as ceramics, glass and metal were decorated with motifs of doves, frolicking deer, leaping gazelles, flowing fountains, female forms, drapes, tassels, feathers and baskets of garlands of fruit. Cubism (cubes and other geometric shapes with an abstract rather than a realistic portrayal of nature) demanded attention after about 1928. Angular forms were stressed. The zig-zag of lightning, the radiance of sunbursts and a feeling of speed were present. The latter was depicted by replicas of greyhounds, autos and airplanes. Most of these were on accessories but furniture had carved drapes, tassels, feathers, baskets of fruits, garlands, sunbursts and other carvings. Orange was a popular color, but purple, bright

greens, gold, silver and reds were dramatic selections also.

The designers were eclectic since they borrowed generously from all sources. Furniture in step shapes was influenced by Aztec temples. The African culture was recalled when blackamoors (figures of dark skinned people) were employed as arm supports for chairs. A dealer at the Indianapolis, Indiana, "Art Deco and Vintage Clothing Show" stated that articles of this era were frequently disguised. Metal furniture was painted with a false walnut grain or fake leopard skin upholstery enhanced chairs. Actually, genuine animal skins were used for fabrics also.

With this background of events that influenced life in the 1920s, 1930s and 1940s, the readers can examine the following chart in order to obtain a general overview of home furnishings from this period.

A restyled oak bookcase of the early 1900s that achieves the Art Moderne feel through the use of polished aluminum, tin plate and leaded glass doors. Bird's-eye maple can be seen on the back panels, 58" wide, 17" deep, 65" high, late 1920s.

An Art Moderne setting showing mohair sofa with carved wooden frame, 75" arm to arm, 32" high, middle 1920s; mahogany veneered coffee table with acid-etched blue mirror top, 30" wide, 17" deep, 16" high, late 1930s; Chrome and onyx standing ash tray, 11" diameter, 28" high, middle 1930s. Accessories include ash tray with Art Moderne pose, 8" wide, 8" high, early 1930s; a pair of red flashed glass Art Moderne fawn tumblers, 7" high, 1940s; mirrored blue glass waste basket, 7" diameter, 11" high, late 1930s.

An Art Moderne setting showing a waterfall vanity with striped walnut veneer on top, sides and drawer fronts, zebrawood veneer between drawers and Macassar ebony veneer below mirror, middle 1930s. Accessories on the vanity are of the period or later and include: pair of crystal lamps with celluloid base; 10" high; ceramic flamingo ash tray (probably of the 1950s) 7" wide, 6" high; crystal heart dish with red flash top and ceramic lady with flowing gown, 10" high. Clothes of the period are pictured in mirror.

An Art Moderne setting showing rattan table with black composition top, 36" square, 30" high and the rattan chair with round back, 21" arm to arm, 29" high, both of the early 1940s. The accessories include a flamingo mirror frame picture (probably of the 1950s), 27" wide, 33" high; a radio lamp with two female figures holding up the light, 10" wide, 21" high; and a bronze female standing on a marble base holding two slag balls.

Furniture Trends in the 1920s, 1930s and 1940s.

Styles do not start and stop on a precise date, but instead, they overlap and run concurrently. Much of the same type furniture appeared throughout the three decades. Urban areas were frequently pace setters while rural areas lagged behind. Consult the chart "Veneer and Their Patterns Introduced in the Catalogues" for a detailed list of woods used.

Years	Woods or Other Materials	Leading Furniture Trends
Early 1920s	Oak lingering but declining in popularity.	Pressed back chairs, claw feet and carvings of grotesques no longer in style.
		Colonial style with scrolled legs, mirror supports and heavy carved posts resembles Late Empire.
		Mission oak with straight, sturdy, unadorned lines.
	Mahogany or walnut veneers, plain, figured or two-tone. Bird's-eye maple veneer.	Chiffoniers and chifforobes popular. Chifforettes introduced. Three-mirror vanity dressers. Pre-woven cane seats frequently on vanity benches, chairs and rockers. Shorter furniture heights. Bow end bed with six feet. Twin or full-sized beds.
Early 1920s	Mahogany and walnut veneers. Oak veneers occasionally.	Case piece on legs. Period furniture copies of Sheraton, Adam, Queen Anne, Hepplewhite, Louis XV and other styles.
		Dust dividers between drawers on case pieces. Drawers had center guides.
	Cedar, selected hardwoods and walnut veneers.	Cedar chests either cedar throughout with wide copper bands on top or cedar interiors with veneered exteriors.
	Tapestry, velour and mohair upholstery. Selected hardwoods.	Massive, overstuffed living room furniture. Very little exposed woods. Chairs with reclining back and footrests.
	Selected hardwoods.	Antique ivory bedroom sets. Painted breakfast sets. Line-decorated kitchen cabinets. Polychrome on buffet mirrors and furniture decorations.
		Decalcomanias, striping and Chinese lacquer designs.
Mid 1920s	Metal	Beds of brass and tubular steel. Metal couches and daybeds.
	Selected hardwoods and veneers. Overlays and inlays.	Smoker stands, humidors. Bedroom, dining sets and tables. Tea or hostess wagons or carts. Telephone sets. Router lines.
Late 1920s	Oak	Hoosier cabinets in golden oak, white and colors.
	Unusual veneers, often of expensive, imported woods such as tigerwood, ebony and avodire. Diamond, book, end to end and other matched veneer patterns.	Almost all types of furniture.
	Stained hardwoods. Walnut and mahogany veneers. Bird's-eye maple veneer overlays.	Magazine holders with floral designs. Radio cabinets and tables. Spinet desks. Martha Washington and Priscilla sewing cabinets. Sectional bookcases.
	Selected hardwoods painted or stained mahongany or walnut.	Windsor chairs and rockers.
Late 1920s	Cedar. Four-way matched butt walnut veneer, either real or imitation.	Cedar chests - many on legs.

Early 1930s	Oak	Roll-top desks and washstands with golden finish. Mission style continues. Arm rockers with large upholstered seats and backs.
	Decorative veneers. Inlaid curly maple. Marquetry.	Book trough, drum, console, davenport, refectory, gateleg, butterfly and extension tables. Spinet desks, Govenor Winthrop secretaries.
		Dresserobe with swinging mirror.
		Buffets with sliding trays for silver.
	Selected hardwoods.	Painted bedroom sets with stenciled decorations. Inexpensive bedroom and dining room furniture with artificial rosewood and fiddleback maple graining.
	Cedar. Walnut veneer with bird's-eye maple, Japanese ash and satinwood veneer overlays. Wood fibre or solid wood decorations.	Cedar chests.
	Metal.	Artificial wood-graining on cots, couches, day beds and washstands. Copper-wash or copper-lined humidors.
		Cheerio liquor cabinets.
		Art Moderne stenciling and striping.
Mid 1930s	Oak.	Dining room and dinette sets with refectory tables.
	Selected hardwoods and veneers.	Duncan Phyfe drop-leaf and drum tables.
	Selected hardwoods.	Two-tone tables combining natural woods and paint.
	Salixwood (black willow) tops.	Art Moderne tables with ribbed legs.
	Chrome, onyx and celluloid.	Case piece handles.
	Chromium, black composition tops, and steel frames.	Art Moderne cocktail and end tables with alcohol-proof finishes.
	Oak and selected hardwoods.	Dome top kitchen cabinets.
	Selected veneers. Veneerite in burl walnut, zebrawood and Orientalwood patterns.	Cellarettes (liquor cabinets). Waterfall bedroom furniture. Vanities with large round mirrors.
	Inlay, marquetry and selected veneers.	Floral designs and router lines.
	Selected hardwoods stained walnut. Upholstery fabrics of angora mohair, jacquard velour, figured or plain tapestry and tapestry friezette.	Living room sets.
	Maple and birch stained maple.	Early American living room and dining room sets.
Late 1930s	Walnut veneer and selected hardwoods.	Low case pieces with body close to floor. Squared lines. Tier tables and nest of tables.
	Selected hardwoods.	Painted breakfast and dinette sets with half round, ribbed legs. Stenciled decorations.
		Waterfall style continues.
	Blonde wood.	Bedroom and dining room sets.
Early 1940s	Oak.	Straight lined china cabinets, credenza buffets and corner cupboards with incised lines. Limed or toasted oak finishes.
	Selected hardwoods or walnut veneer.	Dining room and bedroom sets stained walnut with touches of walnut veneer. Upholstered seats on arm and side chairs. Ribbed lines in legs.
	Leather.	Leather tops on tables with French legs or ribbed, straight legs.
	Selected hardwoods.	Spool and poster beds usually with a walnut finish. Straight lined, undecorated dressers. Frameless mirrors on vanities.
	Bleached walnut and mahogany veneers.	Bedroom sets with blonde finish.

Early 1940s	Maple.	Bunk beds. Colonial refectory tables and Welsh (open) cupboards. Chests-on-chests.
	Maple. Chintz fabric.	Upholstered straight chairs and recliners.
	Selected hardwoods.	Early American living room sets with maple finish.
	Walnut veneer.	Waterfall bedroom and dining room sets. Waterfall effect less pronounced. Electric lights sometimes found in waterfall cedar chests.
	Selected hardwoods.	Dinette sets with striped enamel corner designs and ribbed legs. Open china cabinets.
	Solid walnut, mahogany and cherry. Selected veneers and marquetry inlay.	Copies of late 1700 and 1800 Chippendale, Hepplewhite and Sheraton furniture. Shield and lyre-back chairs.
	Selected hardwoods and veneers. Glass.	Glass over marquetry, matched veneers or carved tops on coffee and cocktail tables with French, Duncan Phyfe or straight legs. Tilt-top, step and tier tables.
	Selected hardwoods and veneers.	Drop-center vanities. Rectangular mirrors with frames. Handleless chests of drawers. Rectangular shaped Mr. and Mrs. dressers with mirrors. Solid panel ends on low beds. New lacquer finish used. Breakfront secretaries, knee-hole and kidney desks.
Mid-1940s	Selected hardwoods.	Tables with mahogany finish and ribbed legs.
Late 1940s	Oak.	Dinette sets with flowers or other designs on tables and chairs. Bedroom and dinette sets with limed oak finish.
	Plastic.	Chairs and sofas with new fabric Korseal. Sectional davenport called four- passenger was divided into two seaters and two chairs. Sofa beds.
	Leather.	Occasional tables with glazed and hand-tooled leather tops.
	Blue glass.	Blue plate glass inset tops on lamp and cocktail tables.
	Selected hardwoods and veneers.	Tier, drum and step tables with ribbed legs. Occasional tables with inlay and marquetry tops. Pembroke, Queen Anne or Duncan Phyfe-style tables.
	Chrome and nickle plated.	Black baked enamel finish on smokers with chrome or nickle touches. Bakelite smoking accessories. Chrome dinette sets.
	Selected hardwoods. Northern hard maple.	Early American living room, dining room and bedroom sets stained maple. Bunk beds.
	Selected hardwoods and veneers.	Waterfall vanities with rectangular mirrors. Double Mr. and Mrs. dressers. Canopy beds and swing beds with a single headboard for twin beds that swung apart. Sectional bedroom sets.
	Metal.	Night stands.
	Fibreboard.	Utilo wardrobe with optional mirror on one or two doors.
	Mahogany veneers and selected hardwoods.	Drop-front credenza desks and blockfront or breakfront secretaries.
	Selected hardwoods and veneers.	Waterfall desks. Whatnots and bookcases with fretwork.
	Bleached and blonde mahogany veneers.	Bedroom and dining room sets, tables and desks.
	Selected hardwood and mahogany and walnut veneers.	Combination record player and radio. Combination record player and television. Record cabinets.
	Cedar and selected veneers.	Waterfall cedar chests. Chippendale and other period styles in cedar chests.
	Selected hardwoods and veneers.	Hostess carts.

Shopping cart, 14″ wide, 12″ deep, 35″ high, middle 1940s. This cart with wooden wheels and frame and the patriotic red, white and blue colors symbolizes World War II when gas was rationed, people walked, metal was needed by the armed forces and rubber tires were not available. The V for Victory, originated by Britain's Prime Minister, Winston Churchill, encourages a united effort in winning the war.

Hostess cart with black lacquer and Oriental scenes, 19″ wide, 30″ deep, 29″ high, 11″ drop leaves, 1940s. This lacquer work in the Chinese manner is called "chinoiserie".

Oak library table with pillar base and scrolled feet, 48″ wide, 28″ deep, 28″ high, 1920s. Heavy scrolls were used on Late Empire furniture of the 1840s. When furniture employed this feature in the 1920s and 1930s, manufacturers advertised the style as "Colonial".

A polychromed (multicolored) base of a metal shoe display stand. Decorations on furniture, metal bases, picture frames, mirrors and lamp bases were often painted with gold, green, red and other colors. Catalogues called this "polychrome".

Occasional table with an "antique" ivory base, a four-piece diamond-matched mahogany veneer top and inlaid design, 18" diameter, 28" high, 1930s. Ribbons and tassels seen on this table were ornamentations of the 1930s.

Windsor-type arm chair made by Quaint American Furniture, Stickly Brothers Company, Grand Rapids, Michigan, 1920s.

In spite of the fact that current fashions attract customers, furniture factories find that certain classical styles from the past are worth reviving. The Windsor chair is a perennial. In an oft-told tale, England's King George III supposedly got caught in a rain storm while out hunting and found refuge in a peasant home. The sturdy chair he sat in easily accommodated his corpulent frame and he wanted a similar one for Windsor Castle; thus, the seat acquired its name. Dissenters say the chair predates this king, who reigned from 1760 to 1820, by half a century, and that it was named for the town, not the castle. The American examples of the chair tend to be more graceful with a multi-spindled construction and a greater splay to the legs. The legs in both English and American types fit directly into the wooden seat instead of having an apron frame. There is normally a splat in the middle of the back of English Windsors with spindles flanking it, and the illustrated example has that characteristic. A paper label, however, indicates that it is not English but a piece made by Quaint American Furniture, Stickley Brothers Company, Grand Rapids, Michigan.

The cabriole leg with its double curve that bulges out at the top, swoops in and sweeps out again at the foot has been around since the early 1700s. Often the top knee was decorated with carving or metal mounts. Its graceful lines, prevalent in the Queen Anne and Louis XV periods, reappeared in Victorian styles after the mid-1800s and were seen again in the 1920s through the 1940s.

Desk with plain-cut walnut veneer top, sides and front, crotch walnut veneer on two side drawers and shell carved cabriole legs, 44" wide, 20" deep, 31" high, late 1940s. The plaque in the drawer lists the furniture dealer as Hathaway's, New York City.

The blockfront desk, a New England native, reached its highest development in Newport, Rhode Island, from 1760-1780. It was made in Connecticut and Massachusetts, too. The front line is broken vertically by three blocks, raised panels, that extend from the bottom to the top, normally terminating with flat arches or in better quality ones, shells within arches. Sometimes there are columns inside a desk that are pulled out to reveal spaces where documents are hidden. This secret feature is present in the Stickley Brothers desk illustrated.

Blockfront desk with paw feet, solid walnut case and four-piece matching crotch walnut veneer on slant front lid, 32″ wide, 18″ deep, 42″ high, 1930s.

George Hepplewhite and Thomas Sheraton both created books on designs that influenced cabinetmakers in their native England and in the United States. Hepplewhite's drawings were published posthumously. These men's works complimented each other and tended to blend so well that there was little distinction between them. A portion of their lives ran concurrently - Hepplewhite (?-1786) and Sheraton (1751-1806). Although both espoused and created similar styles, tapered slender legs and inlay are characteristic of Hepplewhite whereas furniture with carving and straight reeded legs is designated as Sheraton.

A solid mahogany chest of drawers with a Hepplewhite feel, pictured here, includes inlay designs

Hepplewhite-style solid mahogany chest with inlay outlines on drawers and back rail, 42″ wide, 19″ deep, 38″ high, 5″ back rail, 1920s.

and brass bail handles. Because workmanship in the United States was influenced by this English cabinetmaker from approximately 1785 to 1800, the style reappears consistently.

The work of the New York cabinetmaker Duncan Phyfe, in business from approximately 1795 to 1847, has been copied generously. The characteristic Phyfe leg appears on a table shown.

Duncan Phyfe style drop-end occasional table with striped mahogany veneer top, bleached mahogany veneer drawer fronts and selected hardwood base, 30″ wide, 18″ deep, 30″ high, 8″ drop ends, 1930s.

Chests-on-chests are appropriately named. They resemble two chests of drawers, one sitting on top of the other. Mainly they are of English and American derivation from the 1700s and 1800s. Dark hardwoods such as mahogany and walnut were in favor then, but in the late 1930s copies were frequently fashioned in a brown-stained hard maple. The chest-on-chest illustrated has an applied plaque depicting oxen pulling a covered wagon. Although only this one item from a three-piece bedroom set was photographed, the complete set includes a vanity and a bed with a wagon wheel headboard. Since chests-on-chests date back to the 1700s, the term Colonial, as the manufacturer labeled the set, sounds appropriate when applied to such a piece.

Continuing with a western theme, a cowboy-type bunk bed became a popular concept in the late 1940s, especially for boys' rooms. A pictured example has two functions. It could be separated to serve as twin beds or could be stacked to become a single unit. Additional refinements were a ladder with flat rungs, which didn't hurt little feet or cause them to slip and a guard rail that helped keep the occupant from rolling out of the top bunk. These maple beds are called Early American by the manufacturer.

Maple chest-on-chest made by Virginia House, 31″ wide, 17″ deep, 47″ high, 1938.

Maple Early American hutch made by Conant-Ball, 52″ wide, 20″ deep, 75″ high, late 1940s.

Maple bunk bed made by Conant-Ball, 42″ wide, 81″ long, late 1940s.

Maple "Colonial" straight drop-front desk, 40″ wide, 15″ deep in center, 44″ high, 1938.

Conant-Ball Company, Gardner, Massachusetts, created solid maple reproductions of famous Old New England furniture such as twin four-poster beds, night stands, trestle tables, dressing tables, chests and open cupboards. An example of their handiwork, an open cupboard, is illustrated. Customarily there was some combination of drawers and doors at the base while upper shelves were open for the display of china or other objects. Because open cupboards trace their ancestry back to colonial times, copies of the originals are often called Early American. These hutches were introduced in the early 1940s and were generally finished with a mellow brown stain.

Saginaw Furniture Shops of Saginaw, Michigan, had an advertisement in the spring 1933 *Homefurnishing Arts*. The company modestly stated, "Saginaw goes to the trouble, time and expense to obtain more fancy veneers than any other manufacturer. From the Ural Mountains to Australia and around the world to Madagascar it seeks out fine woods." This succinct statement characterizes distinctly the furniture of the Depression days of the 1930s - wide use of exotic veneers.

Chapter Three

Occasional Tables and Stands

Many varieties of stands and tables were available to homemakers in the 1920s, 1930s and 1940s. Often they were designed to meet a specific need. The telephone table is an example.

Early telephones tended to be large, clumsy, wooden instruments that were fastened to walls and had cranks which a caller turned to contact "central", the local operator. While some rural areas retained these wooden crank telephones until the late 1940s, the light weight, upright candlestick 'phone, designed around 1881 to resemble a candleholder, generally replaced them by 1914 in more populated regions.

Telephone table, 8″ wide, 13″ deep, 22″ high; chair, 17″ wide, 29″ high, maple stained with "Butler 900" inscribed on bottom of table, 1946.

Telephone table, 24″ wide, 12″ deep, 31″ high; bench, 16″ wide, 11″ deep, 17″ high, 1920s.

Furniture distributors decided that a telephone needed to have a place of its own. By the mid-1920s,

One-piece telephone bench and stand, 31″ high, selected hardwoods, late 1940s.

a table, a space for the book and a matching bench or chair to accommodate the talker constituted a telephone set. More elaborate styles resembled petite desks. Plain, painted or lacquered with Oriental designs, with separate or attached seats, they became a part of the decor of many homes.

One helpful article was a sewing stand. It was often placed by the sewing machine or next to mother's chair in the living room. There it was handy when she sewed on shirt buttons, darned holey socks or did fancy work as she conversed with the family or listened to the radio in the evening. This stand was not a new form. Instead, it emerged in the late 1700s and early 1800s when Thomas Sheraton's book of furniture designs influenced styles.

In the United States, a small worktable with two receptacles for materials was known as a Martha Washington sewing cabinet. Original examples were made from approximately 1780 to the mid-1800s. Facsimile stands with small central drawers and convex ends that had flat hinged tops that opened reappeared in the 1920s. These copies still bear the name of America's first First Lady. An example is pictured in this chapter.

Priscilla sewing stand, dark mahogany finish over selected hardwoods, 12″ wide, 12″ deep at top, 26″ high, late 1920s.

Martha Washington sewing cabinet of solid mahogany stained dark, 28″ wide, 14″ deep, 29″ high with paper label of Imperial Furniture Company, Grand Rapids, Michigan, and another label guaranteeing that all exterior surfaces are mahogany, late 1920s.

A smaller wooden sewing container that also stood on the floor usually had a handle at the top for transporting and slant lids covering both the enclosed storage units. Manufacturers dubbed it the Priscilla. Also there were diminutive chests of drawers with spool rods to hold thread. Some had compartments where sewing accessories were kept. The various types are illustrated.

Priscilla-type sewing stand, 13″ wide, 11″ deep, 25″ high, early 1930s.

Sewing cabinet of solid mahogany with banding design framing top, 18" wide, 17" deep, 31" high, 1940s.

Martha Washington-type sewing cabinet with plain-cut mahogany veneer on top and side panels and figured mahogany veneer on drawer and doors, 24" wide, 12" deep, 27" high, early 1930s. Dresser lamp with metal gilted stem and polychrome base, 17" high.

Occasional tables abounded. Among these were the short-in-stature coffee and cocktail sizes. Because coffee was a newly imported expensive beverage in colonial times, specialized low tables were not available. During the Victorian Era (1837-1901) tall tables normally held the necessary serving articles. An individual who enjoys furniture from that time span has to cut down a Victorian antique table to the required height if it is to be placed parallel to a sofa. The low coffee or cocktail table was a fresh concept in the 1930s.

Coffee or cocktail table, 24" wide, 16" deep, 21" high, 1930s.

Waterfall front sewing cabinet with plain-cut walnut veneer top, sides and drawer fronts and other parts of walnut stained selected hardwoods, 16" wide, 12" deep, 24" high, late 1930s.

Two factors contributed to the appearance of cocktail tables. As has been stated, in 1920, the Eighteenth Amendment to the Federal Constitution prohibited the manufacture, transportation and sale of alcoholic beverages. The Twenty-first Amendment repealed the Eighteenth in 1933, legalizing liquor except where it was banned by local voters. Since intoxicating beverages were legitimate once again, special tables and cabinets were developed to accommodate them. Because it was difficult to hire servants after World War I and many homes were less spacious, formal dinner parties where guests were seated at tables and served by maids became less common. Instead, stylish cocktail parties where large numbers of people were entertained informally in a smaller space with less help became popular. Drinks and small "finger foods" were available to guests who stood chatting or strolled about mingling with others. The cocktail table entered some homes soon after the prohibition era terminated. Of course, manufacturers realized that many Americans did not imbibe. For them, low tables ranging from 17″ to 21″ in height were advertised as coffee tables. This term was a bland one that did not offend non-drinkers.

Because cocktail and coffee tables were short and normally sat in front of the sofa, their tops could be seen readily and therefore they were frequently decorated. They offered a surface for the exotic veneer work that prevailed in the 1930s. Unusual woods, patterns formed from matching veneers, inlay and marquetry work - all showed up well. A top could be of walnut or stained walnut with the base painted white to provide contrast. Genuine leather tops were hand-tooled, often with a gold outline added. On less expensive examples, a synthetic fabric emulated the real leather. Many tables wore glass tops, some of which had frames and handles so that they were actually trays with a utilitarian as well as a decorative function. In addition, tops with carving in relief (molded or carved ornament or sculpture that is raised above its background) were available. A

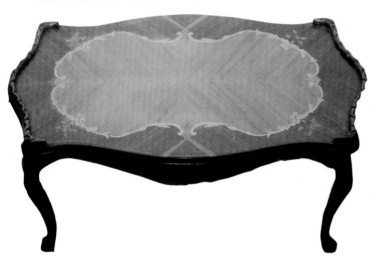

Coffee or cocktail table with natural color four-piece V-matched striped walnut veneer that frames the center bleached striped walnut veneer that is a continuation of the outside pattern. The holly inlay border is accented by four red dyed flowers. 34″ wide, 19″ deep, 17″ high, middle 1930s.

Coffee table with glass top and hand-painted floral design in center of the top, made by the Imperial Furniture Company, 25″ wide, 18″ deep, 18″ high, 1930s.

Coffee or cocktail table with glass tray sitting on V-matched mahogany veneer bordered by walnut veneer and holly inlay and a red and purple floral bouquet. The frame is solid walnut, 27″ wide, 20″ deep, 18″ high, 1927.

Cloverleaf coffee table with leather tooled top and solid mahogany frame, made by the Colonial Manufacturing Company, Zeeland, Michigan, 28″ wide, 19″ high, 1930s.

glass covering provided a flat surface while permitting the carvings of people, scenes, flowers, leaves, fruits, nuts or patriotic emblems such as eagles to be seen.

Coffee or cocktail table with two-piece bleached mahogany center framed by two-tone figured walnut veneer with inlay dividing lines; selected hardwood base, 26" wide, 14" deep, 17" high, 1940s.

Coffee table of solid walnut with hand-carved central design and glass top, 27" wide, 19" deep, 21" high, middle 1930s.

Waterfall coffee or cocktail table with figured walnut veneer top and selected hardwood base, 32" wide, 17" deep, 18" high, late 1930s.

Since shapes, sizes and uses differed, names varied. A home could have a plant stand, tier table, nest of tables, drum, drop-leaf, stand, end table, book trough, console, library or davenport table. Tier types had two or three circular layers graduating in size from the largest at the base to the smallest at the top. Some furniture companies referred to them as dumb waiters, a term usually reserved for a table with trays that revolved on a central shaft. Customarily one stood near the hostess's dining room chair so that additional service, dessert or the like was within easy reach.

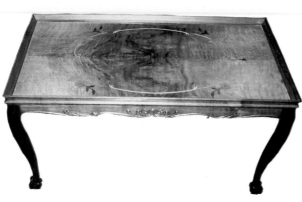

Coffee or cocktail table with four-piece matched crotch walnut veneer top and inlaid designs, appliqued decorations and ball and claw feet, 36" wide, 18" deep, 20" high, dated April 6, 1941 on faded label.

Three-tier plant stand with mahogany veneer tops and solid mahogany frame, 25" wide, 14" deep at bottom, 20" wide, 12" deep in middle, 16" wide, 10" deep at top, 49" high, 1920s.

A nest of tables came to a woman's assistance when she served coffee in the living room. This stack of three or more tables of gradually diminishing sizes fit one beneath the other into a compact single position or could be separated into individual units. When Chinese styles or motifs are imitated, the result is termed chinoiserie whether ceramics, furniture, textiles or other objects are so treated. There is an Oriental scene hand painted on a nest of tables.

Three-tier table with striped mahogany tops, hardwood frame and paw feet, 24″, 20″ and 15″ diameter tiers from bottom to top, 41″ high, late 1930s.

Nest of tables with hand-painted Oriental scene, 20″ wide, 13″ deep, 24″ high for the largest table, late 1930s.

Two-tier Duncan Phyfe-type table with striped mahogany veneer tops and solid mahogany base, 22″ diameter at bottom and 15″ diameter at top, 28″ high, late 1930s.

Nest of tables, the largest of which has drop leaves, with walnut veneer tops and aprons and a solid walnut base, 24″ wide, 15″ deep, 24″ high, 6″ drop leaves, 1940s.

When a table top is hinged to a base or pedestal so that it can be dropped to a vertical position, it is

Tilt-top table of solid mahogany with scalloped top and router lines that originally separated the two tones or colors before the table was stripped, 25" diameter, 27" high, late 1920s.

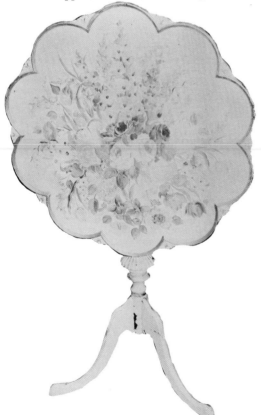

Tilt-top table with hand-painted flowers and a gold trimmed outline, 23" diameter, 27" high folded down to table height, 1920s.

called a tilt-top table. This is an old form dating back to medieval times, and it frequently functioned as a tea serving unit in England and America in the 1700s. It has two obvious advantages. First, it saves space when the top is positioned vertically; and second, the decorated surface shows off well in this position.

Because the shape of one form of a round pedestal table with a deep apron was drum-like, it was called a drum table. To imitate this instrument further, tooled leather tops were sometimes added. Handles in the apron often suggested fake drawers or indicated the presence of real ones. When Thomas Sheraton influenced English furniture styles just prior to and after 1800, the drum table was in vogue. It reemerged in the early 1930s.

Duncan Phyfe-type drum table with tooled-leather top bordered by mahogany veneer, mahogany veneer apron, hardwood base, and brass paw foot ends on legs, 28" diameter, 28" high, late 1930s.

Currently, almost any type of table that fits flush against a wall is called a console table. Customarily, a tall rectangular mirror hung above it. One console table illustrated has flamingo planters on top. These were a fad in the 1950s and one woman was proud of the flamingo design on a mirror because this looking glass was awarded to her mother early in the 1950s as a top premium earned by giving parties to promote cleaning products. It took many points to win this prize. These bird replicas are slightly younger than the three decades spanned in this book. In addition to the consoles, end or arm tables that sat by sofas or chairs frequently had a flat side so they could snuggle up closer to an upholstered piece. While consoles are approximately 31" high, end tables are roughly 24" tall.

Console table with hand-painted floral designs on apron and legs, 39″ wide, 22″ deep, 30″ high, 1930s.

End table that has been stripped of its original darker finish to reveal the natural hardwood base, 24″ wide, 12″ deep, 24″ high, late 1920s. Pot metal night lamp on top of table, 8″ wide, 6″ deep, 9″ high, 1930s.

Console table with two-tone effect through the use of black paint and striped mahogany veneer on top and apron, made by American Woodcraft Corporation, Evansville, Indiana, 1920s.

End table or arm chair table with four-piece matching burl walnut veneer top, selected hardwood apron with sunburst design and solid walnut legs, 24″ wide, 12″ deep, 23″ high, early 1930s.

End table with figured walnut veneer center panel flanked by V-matched striped mahogany veneer and selected hardwood base, 24″ wide, 12″ deep, 23″ high, 1930s.

A table, pictured in this chapter, with delicate, yet strong tapered legs is styled in the manner of George Hepplewhite, an English cabinetmaker circa 1760-1786. Manufacturers have consistently copied the works of masters from the past, some of which are carefully executed to be as near like the original as is feasible. Not all the emulators are that precise even though they enjoy reincarnating the feel of the gentle grace of the Hepplewhite styles. However, the Kittinger Authentique Furniture, inspired by museum originals of the 18th and 19th century, produced quality reproductions as advertised in 1933. The company, located in Buffalo, New York, became the only authorized maker of furniture for Colonial Williamsburg, Virginia.

Hepplewhite drop-leaf table with mottled mahogany veneer top, drop leaves and drawer fronts and solid mahogany base, 17″ wide, 15″ deep, 26″ high, 8″ drop leaves, 1940s.

Kiel Table Company, Milwaukee, Wisconsin, according to information in *Homefurnishing Arts*, fall 1933, sold an elaborately carved Louis XV occasional table with a matched butt walnut veneer top. Their tables were of classical design with abundant carvings. Kiel pieces that were made of solid gumwood and veneered with butt or figured walnut, mottled mahogany or oak swirl were finished as carefully as those of solid mahogany or walnut. Their trademark "Badger" indicated an imitation finish as exemplified by living room tables that were available in English antique walnut, Badger butt walnut, and Badger brown mahogany two-tone finishes.

A change of pace from the usual stand or table is a curio cabinet that holds a family's special mementoes or treasures. Painted furniture was in favor in the 1920s. It was not unusual to add decorative touches through the use of printed transfer designs called decalcomanias (decals), paint applied through stencil perforations, or colorful hand-created garlands. Factory workers completed such details or a creative individual could purchase an unfinished bookcase and apply the desired designs. Tall, narrow pier cabinets that were available in Chinese red or

leaf green held books and bric-a-brac. The Skandia Furniture Company, Rockford, Illinois, offered one in 1928-1929 with ivory crackle finish and hand done decorations.

Curio cabinet with hand-painted floral design on drawers and cornice, 19″ wide, 12″ deep, 66″ high, 1930s.

One space-saving drop-leaf table bears a noble name. Supposedly, in or around 1770, the Countess of Pembroke desired a rather small table - perhaps a breakfast size. In an effort to please her, the Earl of Pembroke consulted the noted English cabinetmaker, Thomas Chippendale. A rectangular table with drop leaves that were supported by brackets when raised and with a drawer at the end apparently satisfied the countess. This story states that, in honor of the earl, the table was named for him and the Pembroke table was born. A few decades later other craftsmen created examples in the Hepplewhite and Sheraton manner; thus, the Pembroke table was accepted by the English gentry. Copies appeared through the years and some factories produced them in the 1940s.

Butterfly table sounds as if it should have a connection with the flying insect of that name. It does, because it is petite with two drop leaves that are each suspended by a swinging bracket resembling a butterfly wing. It is thought to be a table developed in the United States. Maple butterfly tables were prevalent during the 1940s when emphasis on maple furniture began to emerge. However, it was a frequent practice in the 1930s, as the pictured example shows, to paint a base while leaving the top surface in its natural wood tone, usually walnut.

Duncan Phyfe-type drop-leaf black lacquered table with Oriental design accents and gold trim, made by Imperial Furniture Company, Grand Rapids, Michigan, 20″ wide, 18″ deep, 27″ high, 8″ drop leaves, 1920s.

Drop-leaf child-size table with original two tone white painted base and four-piece striped mahogany matching veneer on top and striped mahogany on drop leaves, 18″ wide, 10″ deep, 23″ high, 8″ drops, 1930s.

Swinging on a gate once was a childish pastime. A gate-leg refers to a table where the drop leaf is upheld by a supporting leg that swings out in gate-like fashion when needed. Stretchers are a part of the structure. Some authorities claim it's a swing leg when there is no stretcher. If a table is painted and a narrow streak of a contrasting color is applied, it is referred to as striping, and gate-legs at times received this treatment.

Pembroke table with plain-cut mahogany veneer top and drop leaves, figured mahogany drawer front and solid mahogany base made by the Colonial Art Furniture Shop, Grand Rapids, Michigan, 15″ wide, 22″ deep, 27″ high, 10″ drops, 1940s.

Gate-leg table with original enameled finish, 34″ wide, 12″ deep, 29″ high, 15″ drop leaves, early 1920s.

It is amazing that tables could retain an identity of their own when such a vast number of the occasional kinds were made. Legs were gracefully curved in the cabriole fashion so that they protruded at the knee, swept inward and then swung out at the foot. Turnings contrasted sharply with delicate, plain-appearing tapered versions. There were four or six legs or a pedestal. Stretchers were turned, plain or decorated. In the late 1930s and in the 1940s, the legs of fashionable tables were straight with parallel grooves running up and down their surface. These are referred to as channeled or ribbed.

Rich veneers laid out in interesting patterns or of different varieties of woods so that their light and dark shades contrasted were a special emphasis of the 1930s. Dainty inlay work added pleasing outlines and designs. When this sort of work covered an extensive area such as a whole top, it was called marquetry. When pallid woods were dyed, colorful decorations such as floral bouquets could bloom on the surface of tables. Pale holly, satinwood and tulipwood were frequently used to achieve such results. All three are light in color, have no figure and are evenly grained so they accept stain and dye readily.

When a friend desired to refinish a table he received from his grandparents, it was difficult to encourage him to do so because he felt that the bright flowers would fade away when attacked by the paint remover. Instead, their reds and yellows bloomed forth with renewed beauty because the dye that was used in this instance was not effected by the chemicals in the remover.

Octagonal occasional table with wheel-like base and hand-painted Oriental pagodas and peacock on top, 30″ wide, 30″ deep, 30″ high, 1920s.

Occasional table that has been stripped of its original finish. Shows a bleached figured walnut veneer top flanked by burl walnut veneer ends, a burl walnut veneer oval panel and a selected hardwood base, 34″ wide, 21″ deep, 31″ high, late 1920s.

Occasional table with four-piece butt walnut matched veneer and inlay design on top, hardwood base, carved apron and French legs, 30″ wide, 20″ deep, 30″ high, 1930s.

Occasional table with veneer top enhanced with Macassar ebony triangular and shield designs, 35″ wide, 22″ deep, 30″ high, 1920s.

Occasional table of selected hardwoods that has been stripped of its original color was made by the Kiel Furniture Company, Milwaukee, Wisconsin, 37″ wide, 22″ deep, 30″ high, 1920s.

The transition from the predominant use of walnut and mahogany veneers in the early 1920s to the use of exotic imported and domestic veneers can be seen by consulting furniture catalogues of the late 1920s throughout the 1930s. By 1923 the trend toward variety was evident because burl or butt walnut, rosewood, figured or bird's-eye maple and tulipwood veneers appeared as overlays. "Selected" and "figured" were terms that denoted any kinds of walnut or other veneers. Gold or ebony lines often provided decorations. A few years later matched butt walnut was combined with mottled mahogany and blistered maple. Diamond-matched patterns were becoming prominent.

· By the 1930s a multitude of veneer patterns were available for the tops of occasional tables and were described by manufacturers as four-way matched, butt walnut veneer; quarter-sawed gum; diamond-shaped Oriental walnut center and burl madrone ends; combination walnut and gum; walnut with V-matched bubinga center and ends with an inlaid holly stripe; Tasmanian blackwood and padauk with an inlaid holly border; and quilted maple with a diamond-matched walnut center and ends and inlaid holly stripes.

Octagonal and drum tables were present. The long davenport tables, measuring approximately 16″ x 44″, that customarily stood behind a davenport were frequently of either plain or quarter-sawed gum with a walnut finish. A more expensive type was of solid mahogany, combined with walnut or gum. Quite frequently router line decorations appeared and separated the different woods used on a table top.

In the mid-1930s, veneerite decorations appeared on inexpensive furniture and resembled shell-figured butt walnut bordered by zebrawood. The veneerite, a facsimile made to look like true veneer, appeared

fakey. Some simulated burl walnut and Orientalwood. Genuine veneers included diamond-matched tigerwood fronts flanked by butt walnut, Circassian walnut, inlaid striped walnut strips, rosewood, claro crotch and colobra or colobra crotch.

Veneers and veneer patterns listed for the early 1940s included New Guinea wood, four-way matched burl or butt walnut, prima vera, fiddleback mahogany, paldao and claro. As a whole, a less vivid, more gentle use of veneering began to appear.

The United State's energies were devoted to World War II production from 1941 throught 1945 and a limited amount of furniture was produced. Following the war, factories had to reconvert to peace-time activities.

Throughout the 1920s, 1930s and 1940s, shapes varied greatly. Octagonal forms, oval, rectangular, scalloped, clover leaf, round - the choice was wide. Individual taste was catered to because even the aprons featured different details. By inspecting the pictures and reading the descriptions beneath them, it is possible to notice some of these distinctions.

Some catalogues classify what is usually considered a game or card table as a console since its flat side can be backed against a wall. The Elite Furniture Company, Jamestown, New York, called theirs a "folding console table." The leaf on these tables is versatile enough to assume various positions. It can stand upright against a wall. It can be folded over the table top to form a double surface or when the top and leaf are pivoted on the base, it can be opened flat to form an extended surface for playing games. Now, that's really a multi-position table.

Game tables are not new. They've been around for nearly three hundred years. The example illustrated has a Duncan Phyfe-style pedestal base.

Game table or console table (as it was called in the catalogues) with figured mahogany veneer top and apron and selected hardwood base, 32″ wide, 15″ deep, 29″ high, late 1930s.

41

Originally Phyfe made furniture with a refined air. That was before his clients sought the fashionable Late Empire styles that brought a heaviness to his work. His game tables, after which the one shown is patterned, had a delicate, graceful appearance.

Many companies manufactured tables with the Duncan Phyfe leg. The lyre with its curving frame and its strings to pluck to produce music pleased Phyfe and he copied its lines with a delicate touch on chair backs and table bases. His emulators in the 1920s, 1930s and 1940s revived this shape and attached his name to their efforts. Often leaf carvings on table feet are a Phyfe inherited characteristic. This skillful cabinetmaker liked to work with mahogany, shifting his allegiance later to rosewood. Imitations in this period are frequently of walnut veneer.

Imperial Furniture Company of Grand Rapids, Michigan, manufactured a Phyfe inspired card table with a revolving top, carved pedestal and brass claw feet. A commode they made had a rounded front with an inlaid design of a woman and a harp in the center of the door. The woods this company used included mahogany, walnut, oak, chestnut, maple, pine, gumwood and various decorative veneers such as hurawood, satinwood, pollard oak and Macassar ebony. Standard finishes were Tudor mahogany highlighted, walnut highlighted, brown mahogany not highlighted, chestnut highlighted, maple highlighted and pine highlighted. A genuine waterproof lacquer finish was used. Each article of furniture carried a tag that enumerated the woods utilized in its manufacture. F. Stuart Foote founded the company in 1903 and their trademark was the well known green shield.

Mersman, a manufacturer located in Celina, Ohio, produced a good quality brand a family with a moderate income could afford. All of their table tops are of five-ply construction. Among the woods most used for table tops, veneers and trims were brown mahogany; plain, burl, rotary-cut and butt jointed walnut; rosewood; blistered maple; bird's-eye maple; zebrawood veneers; ebony; redwood burls; satinwood and Russian oak. Marquetry inlays were frequently incorporated in their designs.

Occasional table made of selected hardwoods stained walnut, 15″ square, 28″ high, 1930s.

Occasional table with tripod base, figured mahogany veneer top, solid mahogany scalloped edge and selected hardwood base made by Mersman, 24″ diameter, 27″ high, 1930s.

Waterfall occasional table with selected hardwood base and narrow mahogany veneer strip in the center of the top separating two figured walnut veneer panels, 26″ wide, 14″ deep, 24″ high, early 1940s.

Occasional table with figured and striped mahogany veneer top and inlaid designs on each corner, a selected hardwood base, French legs and applied decorations on apron, 17″ square, 26″ high, 1930s.

Lyre-base occasional table with plain-cut walnut veneer top and gallery and selected hardwood base made by Mersman, 24″ wide, 18″ deep, 26″ high, 1920s.

Occasional table with plain-cut walnut veneer top and a selected hardwood base, 18″ wide, 15″ deep, 27″ high, 1940s.

Occasional table with leather-tooled top and selected hardwood base, 14″ diameter, 20″ high, 1930s.

When an end table has a slanted V-shaped base, it is known as a book trough, but it is called a book rack also. Many were constructed from hardwood and stained walnut or mahogany. Usually, book troughs were a common, inexpensive, yet useful piece of furniture. Because of this, they are still easy to acquire today and can be found at garage sales or flea markets.

End table with book trough, 24″ wide, 12″ deep, 25″ high, late 1920s.

Occasional stand with striped mahogany veneer top, sides and drawer fronts and selected hardwood base, 19″ wide, 13″ deep, 29″ high, 1940s. Tiffany-type lamp on top of stand with red spun glass shade, 25″ high.

An Art Moderne feel is achieved when one sees a table where two round shelves are suspended in a wooden framework and a round base provides stability. Art Moderne styles differed from the norm and might not be selected by buyers with conservative, conventional tastes. Colored blue mirrors appeared as tops. Chromium, frequently shortened to chrome, plated steel frames and black composition tops with

Occasional table with black lacquer finish and a gold and floral designed top made by Quaint Furniture of Character, Stickley Brothers, Company, Grand Rapids, Michigan, 19″ wide, 13″ deep, 24″ high, 1920s.

Art Moderne two-tier stand of solid walnut, 15″ wide, 8″ deep, 27″ high, 1930s.

an alcohol-proof finish, were present on cocktail tables and end tables. The Howell Company, Geneva, Illinois, was known as one maker of chromsteel furniture. They marketed a Howellite red top table with a red metal apron.

In contrast to the above styles, Baker Furniture, Inc., established in 1890 in Allegan, Michigan, and moved to Holland, Michigan, in 1933, has long been associated with authentic copies from the past. A table labeled "Milling Road Furniture, division of Baker Furniture, Inc." is an example depicted. One of the company's undated catalogues mentions a 1950 design that is not of the time period covered in this book. However, it does explain how quality products are produced. The company stated that "the skilled hands of the individual craftsman" contribute subtleties and enduring quality. Ignoring the short cuts mass production permits, "Baker is one of the few remaining strongholds of hand workmanship." Their designs represent the best from Europe or the Far East, each is authentic and wherever possible, adheres to the original in all details. Usually the woods are those found in the original. This necessitates research and much searching to find exotic woods from all over the world. According to the catalogue, "Baker cabinetmakers, carvers and finishers are chosen for their commitment to excellence."

Table desk with straight-cut walnut veneer top and antique white base made by Milling Road Furniture, a division of Baker Furniture, Inc. 48″ wide, 24″ deep, 30″ high, 1940s.

France provided the inspiration for the 1940s two-tone Baker table illustrated. Its top is walnut veneered while the base is painted an antique white. The flowing curves of the cabriole legs, a handleless middle drawer flanked by two drawers with ornate handles and gold outlines on molded panels are characteristic of the decorative qualities of French furniture.

A stand that gained prominence in the 1920s was the smoker or smoking stand. When an enclosed copper or copper coated tin-lined section with a moisture pad was added to keep tobacco fresh, a humidor resulted. The variety of woods utilized on one piece typified the construction techniques of the late 1920s and 1930s. A picture is almost painted by the descriptive names assigned to various veneers. Who can forget that zebrano or zebrawood is named for the zebra, that swift African relative of a horse whose dark stripes stand out against a tawny or white

Smoking stand with two portable standing ash trays, 16″ wide, 11″ deep, 31″ high, 1920s.

Smoking stand with striped walnut veneer top, zebrano wood veneer on door, bird's-eye maple apron and selected hardwood base, 19″ wide, 12″ deep, 26″ high, 1927.

background. Some imaginative person saw the tiny eyes of birds in the pattern of bird's-eye maple and named it accordingly. Some authorities state that this spotted look results when buds are embedded too deeply to penetrate the bark to reach the surface of the tree. Although this figure occurs in other woods, it is more commonly found in maple. The combination of such veneers adds character to some smokers.

In the early 1930s some smokers were of birch, gum and metal and had decorative decals on their fronts applied over burl or butt walnut panels. More expensive examples had satinwood inlays. An Oriental design on one stand is different because, in addition to the green, red, yellow and black tones of the garden and building picture there is a "done on purpose" crackle appearance. This finely cracked surface gives the feeling of age even though it is done too precisely to faithfully copy the natural irregularities of crazing found on old wood finishes.

Smoking stand with enamel green crackled finish and Oriental hand-painted design on door front, 11″ wide, 10″ deep, 28″ high, 1920s.

While one smoker has a pagoda-type temple building in the background, another has a religious building with a Moslem feel - a pointed dome mosque with the figure of an apparent Turk and a palm tree nearby. Perhaps this picture is in keeping with China's history as the Turkish Moslems fought the Mongols. (Inner Mongolia is a part of China.) The scene, however, is not typical of the pagodas, garden and Chinese people found on reproduced Oriental lacquer designs. While the possibility remains that the artist merely chose something he liked to depict

without trying to be historical, Turkish tobacco is known and the Turks introduced fine cigarettes to the British.

Smoking stand with black lacquer finish and hand-painted scene on front showing a smoking Moselm Turk, 17″ wide, 11″ deep, 29″ high, 1920s.

Smoking stand that has been stripped of its original finish was made by Metal Stamping Corporation, Streator, Illinois. This model is marked "Smoker No. 327", 10″ square, 31″ high, 1920s.

46

Smoking stand that has been stripped of its original finish has a striped mahogany veneer top and door front and selected hardwood base, 21″ wide, 14″ deep, 29″ high, 1920s.

Smoking stand with straight-cut walnut veneer top, crotch walnut veneer door front and painted base, 18″ wide, 11″ deep, 28″ high, 1930s.

Smoking stand with figured walnut veneer top, sides and door panel, a selected hardwood base and a painted flower design on front door outlined with router lines, 13″ wide, 9″ deep, 30″ high, 1930s.

Smoking stand made of selected hardwoods stained walnut and a hand-painted floral design on door. This is a Cushman smoker made in North Bennington, Vermont, 15″ wide, 10″ deep, 25″ high, 1930s.

Onyx, a type of agate with alternating layers of color, frequently is used as a semi-precious stone. On occasion devotees of Art Moderne incorporated it in their designs and it enhanced many smoking stands of this period.

Art Moderne standing ash trays with accents of color and onyx, 29″ high, middle 1930s.

A combination piece is a handy space saver. An Art Moderne end table features an inner humidor compartment for a smoker and a magazine rack base

Art Moderne combination smoking stand, end table and magazine rack with a four-piece walnut figured veneer center panel on top flanked by V-matched mahogany veneer panels that are separated by veneerite strips. A two-piece V-matched mahogany veneer is on the door. Inside the door is a copper-wash metal-lined compartment to hold the smoking supplies, 24″ wide, 11″ deep, 22″ high, late 1930s.

to make it a three-in-one-unit utilitarian piece. Composition handles and strips of imitation inlay called veneerite were characteristic of inexpensive furniture in the 1930s. Veneerite or router lines stained dark were used as dividers between different veneers on a surface.

Smoking stand with V-matched striped mahogany door front and mahogany and selected hardwood body, 14″ wide, 12″ deep, 24″ high, late 1930s. An Art Moderne radio lamp on the top shows a woman with hunting bows caressing two fawns, 9″ wide, 3″ deep, 10″ high.

It is difficult to believe that in one of their catalogues, Quaint Furniture, Stickley Brothers Company, Grand Rapids, Michigan, offered tea wagons with at least eighteen applied finishing touches in soft enamel colors. Because interior decorators liked to contrast, not match, accessory items, the Stickley ad stated these colorful carts could brighten sun rooms, dining areas, living rooms or boudoirs. If you didn't want birds, berries, butterflies, flowers or Oriental decorations, many new and original hand-done designs were turned out daily. If none of these appealed to you, you could buy a plain one and decorate your own.

At times a distinction was made between different forms. A tea wagon had a tray top and one shelf. A serving wagon shown in a catalogue had three shelves. Also available was a tea table. All three had the glass tray tops, some had one drawer and handles for pushing, if present, were stationary or collapsible to fold down to save space. Movable hostess wagons often had casters rather than two big rear wheels. Names seem to be interchangeable, however, partly because all companies did not use similar definitions. Tea cart or tea wagon is usually accepted as the generic name.

It can be readily seen from this chapter's description of tables and stands that the multitude of types manufactured in the 1920s, 1930s and 1940s gave the buying public a wide selection.

Serving wagon of solid oak with glass top, 33″ wide, 19″ deep, 32″ high, 1920s. Three-piece Manning-Bowman serving set on top shelf, early 1930s; green panther planter and lamp on middle shelf, late 1940s; Forest green Anchorglass pitcher and glasses on bottom shelf; a Maxfield Parish influenced picture, probably from a calendar, in gold and artificially grained frame, 19″ wide, 23″ high, middle 1930s.

Tea cart with striped mahogany veneer top, drop leaves and bottom shelf and selected hardwood body, 26″ wide, 16″ deep, 11″ drop leaves, 30″ high, early 1920s.

Tea wagon with crackle finish, Oriental hand-painted designs and figures and a removable glass tray top, 26″ wide, 18″ deep, 29″ high, 1920s.

Hostess wagon with red lacquered finish and hand-painted Oriental designs on top, drop leaves and bottom shelf and a removable glass tray, 16″ wide, 26″ deep, 10″ drop leaves, 30″ high, early 1920s.

Hostess wagon with figured mahogany veneer apron, top and bottom shelf and solid mahogany legs, 27″ wide, 19″ deep, 27″ high, 1930s.

Tea cart of solid cherry with French legs, 30″ wide, 20″ deep, 10″ drop leaves, 30″ high, 1930s.

Chapter Four

A Place To Eat

Before the general acceptance of fast foods, drive-ins, frozen foods, TV dinners, prepared mixes and an excess of wives joining the labor force, the kitchen with its cooking aromas and mother's presence did seem to be the heart of the house. Anything that helped save steps and promoted convenience was great in those "It was made from scratch" days. That's probably why the description of kitchen cabinets sound so terrific. In 1923-1924 the Montgomery Ward catalogue headlines read, "Now you can say good-by to kitchen drudgery! . . . This cabinet makes your day's work lighter and shorter . . . Fingertip convenience that replaces footsteps."

These cabinets were sanitary and easy to clean. There were swinging dust-proof sugar jars, flour bins and sifters; pull-outs including shelves, porcelain top work space, breadboards and choppers. Bread drawers with ventilated metal tops, files for recipes and bills, coin slots and partitioned drawers were incorporated. Ward's spring and summer 1929

Sellers kitchen cabinet, tan oak with green trim, No. 3462 as indicated on the back of cabinet, 40″ wide, 25″ deep, 72″ high, late 1920s.

Hoosier kitchen cabinet, 36″ wide, 23″ deep, 68″ high, late 1920s.

catalogue has a page of colored pictures that stand out amid the black and white format. It shows cabinets available in warm golden oak, snowflake white, modern French gray, rich old ivory or new spring green. These Hoosier-type gems were blooming out in attractive attire. The theme remained consistent when the 1933 "wish book" (catalogue) exclaimed, "Every woman wants the step-saving, work-saving convenience of a modern kitchen cabinet."

Evidentally these special cupboards were better than a maid because you didn't have to feed or clothe them. The new system of paying by installments lured many families to buy.

Since many of these popular drudgery savers were made in the Hoosier state at New Castle, Indiana, by the Hoosier Manufacturing Company, the generic title for these cupboards became "Hoosier" cabinets. Sellers & Sons Company of Elwood, makers of the Sellers Kitchen Cabinet, June Bride and Kitchen Maid; Coppes Bros. & Zook of Nappanee (Nappanee Kitchen Cabinets); Ingram Richardson Manufacturing Company, Frankfort; Wasmuth Endicott Company of Andrews; Boone and Greencastle were other known names in the state.

Hoosier-type kitchen cabinet, limed oak, 39″ wide, 26″ deep, 72″ high, late 1920s.

It is more meaningful to a purist when a Hoosier retains its original white factory paint and floral

decorations. Identifying markings at times occur on metal handles, instruction cards or other paper labels and should be preserved. Finding a tag such as the one on a Sellers Kitchen Cabinet that states, "Tan oak, green trim" establishes its natal coloring. These work center storage units became more colorful in the 1920s and 1930s than their earlier oak, white or gray factory-painted ancestors. Decals and stencils added designs and fret work on the doors became whimsical when it featured an outline of a coffee pot as seen in a pictured example.

Hoosier-type kitchen cabinet, enameled finish, 40″ wide, 32″ deep with porcelain work area extended, 70″ high, late 1920s.

In keeping with new trends in the mid-1930s, the squared lines of the old Hoosiers were at times replaced by a dome that gave the cabinet an Art Moderne appearance. Generally, traditional features such as the pull-out porcelain work area, flour and sugar containers, bread drawer and the storage units remained even though the frame was streamlined.

After all those hard working Hoosier types, it's novel to see the plain oak kitchen cabinet pictured here. It has Bakelite handles. In 1909, this synthetic resin was named in honor of its inventor, American chemist Leo. H. Baekeland. Bakelite helped introduce the use of plastic wares. When the original handles on a case piece, such as a kitchen cabinet, were fashioned from Bakelite, it is immediately evident that the furniture is a twentieth century piece.

Art Moderne kitchen cabinet, oak construction, 40″ wide, 26″ deep, 73″ high, middle 1930s.

Breakfast sets and dinette sets are similar except in addition to the table and four chairs, the latter usually had a buffet or server. Frequently, there was a cozy "breakfast nook", generally an alcove, where the family ate instead of in the formal dining room. Small tables and chairs of elm or oak were used in such areas. Tables were often of ash, but many were of solid oak, although some had veneered oak tops. These represented an entirely new style from that which was prevalent in the late 1800s and the start

One of two oak chairs from a three-piece breakfast set, 36″ high, 1920s.

Kitchen cabinet, oak construction, that was originally finished in white enamel, 32″ wide, 16″ deep, 70″ high, 1930s.

Oak drop-leaf table from a three-piece breakfast set including two chairs, 37″ wide, 23″ deep, 9″ drop leaves, 30″ high, 1920s.

of the 1900s. At the turn of the century, the pieces tended to be thick and stocky. Tables had stout pedestal bases or big bulbous legs. Chairs frequently had tall backs with designs pressed into their slats. Another style, called Mission, emphasized straight sturdy, clean, plain and unadorned lines. In comparison, the new sets appeared dainty. In addition, the treatment of their surfaces differed. They were not finished with a golden oak glow, dark antique stain or ammonia or smoke vapors. Instead, color showed forth.

Decalcomanias (decals), stencils or free-hand painting supplied the floral, fruit or geometric touches, usually at the corners of the tables and on the backs of chairs. Both the table and chair legs often had highlights of paint on their turnings. Striping around the edge with a band of contrasting color or shading was common. Applying one hue of paint over the entire surface and then, after it dried, blending in a darker shade along the seat or table edge to create a two-tone effect was another technique employed.

One 1927 catalogue issued by Chittenden-Eastman, a wholesale distributor, advertised as the largest in the world, presented a kaleidoscope of the furniture produced by approximately 120 companies. Breakfast sets consisted of four chairs and a table.

It is delightful to read the descriptions of the colors available. Is your preference seagull gray, Chinese red, canary yellow, kingfisher blue or pheasant green? A vivid selection was possible. Darker strokes accentuated the rungs. The distributor's 1931 catalogue listed an antique walnut finish with Art Moderne stenciling. Striping in red, black, green and yellow was present on chair rails and chair legs.

In 1929 the Phoenix Chair Company, Sheboygan, Wisconsin, produced complete sets for breakfast alcoves and apartment dining rooms. Their hues were described as solid oak finish in acorn walnut, London smoke, salmon, ash gray, seal brown or fawn. Other finishes available were silver gray, green parchment, ivory parchment and violet shaded.

Turned splayed (slanted out) legs were characteristic of the 1920s and 1930s tables and chairs and are one clue in dating these pieces. These sets, combined with the bright touches that dressed up the Hoosiers, created cheery kitchens.

Arm chair from a four-piece breakfast set, 21″ arm to arm, 35″ high, late 1930s.

Oak extension table from a four-piece breakfast set including one arm chair and two side chairs, 44″ wide, 32″ deep, 8″ drop leaves, 30″ high, late 1930s.

One of two oak chairs from a three-piece breakfast set, 34″ high, 1930s.

Oak extension table from a three-piece breakfast set including two side chairs, 43" wide, 30" deep, 30" high, 1930s.

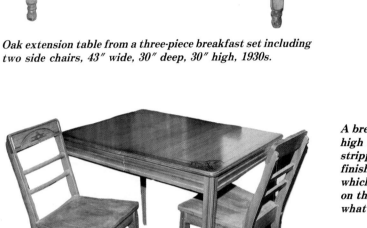

A breakfast set including an oak extension table, 42" wide, 32" deep, 30" high and four oak side chairs, 35" high, 1930s.

A breakfast set including two benches, 53" long, 18" deep, 36" high and a table, 48" wide, 26" deep, 30" high that has been stripped down to pine from the original painted and decaled finish, early 1940s. A complete service for six in Fiesta Ware, which was introduced in 1936 and discontinued in 1973, sits on the table. This type of a breakfast set was often found in what was called the "breakfast nook" next to the kitchen.

Sellers and Company produced breakfast sets as well as their line of cabinets. A label beneath the table top with orange and black striping reads "Sellers Crystal Oak." Many tables had porcelain tops and drop leaves. A mutation shown has drop leaves of maple veneer with only the center top of porcelain.

Benches with tables, instead of chairs and a table, frequently occupied breakfast nooks. Usually, they were bolted in place for stability and a family member arriving late for the meal had to slide over the laps of others to get an inside seat. If someone occupying an inner position had to leave the table early, this was distruptive. It was almost as difficult as trying to reach the aisle from the middle of a row of theatre seats.

A table and its matching benches are illustrated. They have been refinished to reveal their pine heritage. Ordinarily they came from the factory painted and were not intended to look pine pale unless an individual bought an unfinished set to paint and decorate with floral bouquets, colored lines or fruit designs. On the top of the table is a complete set of Fiesta ware for six. This currently collectible ware was made by Homer Laughlin Company, Newell, West Virginia, from 1936 to 1973.

Oak drop-leaf breakfast table, 36" wide, 21" deep, 10" drop leaves, 30" high, 1920s.

These surfaces were decorated with colored edges and floral designs. Some included extension leaves and one or two drawers. Straight legs with dark accents in their vertical grooves were common.

Since furniture makers sought inspiration from the past, they frequently combined and borrowed ideas generously as they designed their "new furniture." This eclectic tendency was present in the 1920s and dining room sets were assigned names such as Tudor, Spanish Renaissance, Renaissance, Queen Anne or the like. Quite often, however, a factory's interpretation deviated from the original. In expensive furniture, quality companies sought to be precise in their attempts to reproduce exact copies of the works of master craftsmen.

Sellers extension table is marked "Crystal White - Oak" on the bottom and has ring on the end to pull so the table can be extended, 42″ wide, 30″ deep, 31″ high, 1920s.

Host chair with blistered maple veneer splat and Orientalwood veneer top rail, 23″ arm to arm, 40″ high, late 1920s. Part of an eight-piece set including five side chairs, a buffet and a table.

Maple drop-leaf kitchen table with porcelain top and one drawer, 20″ wide, 36″ deep, 12″ drop leaves, 31″ high, 1930s.

Buffet with plain-cut walnut veneer top and sides, burl walnut veneer doors and bottom drawer and blistered maple veneer top drawer and panels, 66″ wide, 22″ deep, 36″ high, late 1920s. Part of an eight-piece set including one host chair, five side chairs and a table.

Drop-leaf kitchen table with decorated enamel porcelain top, a drawer at each end, and a painted wooden base, 40″ wide, 24″ deep, 31″ high, 1930s.

Dining room table with plain-cut walnut veneer top and selected hardwood base, 60″ wide, 42″ deep, 31″ high, late 1920s. Part of an eight-piece set including one host chair, five side chairs and a buffet.

One fact does stand out. Mainly, the sideboards from the last half of the 1800s were solidly built, their frames extending to the floor with hardly any exposed leg to stand on. At times, casters were about all that kept them from sitting flat on the floor. This was not true of the 1920s and 1930s. Legs on furniture (and on women who had modestly covered theirs with long skirts even as late as 1918) were suddenly featured. Heavy, turned versions were often

termed Renaissance while slightly less massive examples were called Tudor. A set with gently curved cabriole legs became Queen Anne. The period names assigned were determined by the shape of the legs.

Queen Anne-style buffet with cabriole legs, striped mahogany veneer on top and sides, fiddleback mahogany veneer on drawers and doors and burl mahogany veneer oval panels on doors and solid mahogany legs, 1920s. Part of a set including six side chairs.

When oak was the ruling wood between 1895 and 1920, some extension tables were square with bulbous legs, but heavy extension pedestal tables were more frequently seen. From the 1920s on, rectangular shapes became prominent. One form was the refectory table. In the Middle Ages, circa 476 A.D.-1450 A.D., dining rooms in monastaries were called refectories. Therefore, it seemed only natural that these long narrow tables where monks sat to eat were called refectory tables.

Later, a refectory, or draw table, was constructed with a double top. The lower level was divided in half so that it pulled out and up to add to the length to accommodate more diners.

It was possible to purchase individual items from sets. If a family needed chairs and a table but could not afford a buffet, the latter might be acquired at a later date. Various companies produced similar wares and stores stocked merchandise from different sources. A family, then, could conceivably purchase pieces that nearly matched by selecting dining room furniture separately. In one case, a buffet that the owners thought matched the table bears the name of a different manufacturer. The table label reads "B Walter & Co., Inc. Wabash, Indiana, U.S. pat #1736533", a number issued in 1929. This date indicated that the table was either made in that year or sometime during the following years covered by the patent. The tag on the back of the buffet is "Kent-Coffey Manufacturing Company Furniture Manufacturers Lenoir North Carolina".

Queen Anne-style side chair with cabriole legs, walnut veneer splat, solid walnut top rail and selected hardwoods made by Angert Brothers, Cincinnati, Ohio, 1920s. Part of a set including five additional side chairs and a buffet.

Draw table with striped walnut veneer center panel and selected hardwood base made by B. Walter & Company, Inc., Wabash, Indiana, 62" wide, 38" deep, 17" extension, 30" high, 1929. Part of a two-piece set including buffet.

Buffet with striped walnut veneer top and sides, butt walnut veneer drawer and door fronts and selected hardwood base, 68" wide, 21" deep, 36" high, made by Kent-Coffey Manufacturing Company, Furniture Manufacturers, Lenoir, North Carolina, late 1920s. Part of a two-piece set including draw table.

organization waned and he withdrew in 1873. It was then that the firm was incorporated as Berkey & Gay Furniture Company. It grew to become one of the most famous Grand Rapids plants.

Host chair with striped mahogany veneer back panel and selected hardwoods, 27" arm to arm, 43" high, 1926. Part of a nine-piece set including five side chairs, a table, a buffet, and a court cupboard made by Berkey & Gay Furniture Company, Grand Rapids.

A chart entitled, "Patent Serial Numbers and Dates Issued - 1920-1950" is included in this book.

Consider the story of Grand Rapids, Michigan, the furniture capital of the United States in the 1800s. Picture loggers hewing trees in the forest so that horse-drawn sleds could carry enough logs across the winter's snow to supply the yearly needs of the factories. Imagine salesmen hawking their furniture wares from trains at towns along the railroad route. That's history.

One of the famous quality furniture makers in Grand Rapids was Berkey & Gay Furniture. This company traces its origin to 1859 when Julius Berkey and James Eggleston united to construct furniture. As the years progressed, Julius Berkey had a procession of associates including his brother, William A., and in 1863 the firm became Berkey Bros. & Company In 1866, George W. Gay purchased half of William's share and the name switched to Berkey Brothers & Gay. When William founded the Phoenix Furniture Company in 1870, his interest in the old

Buffet with striped mahogany veneer on top and sides, V-matched mahogany veneer on doors, diamond-matched mahogany veneer on bottom drawer, Carpathian elm burl on top drawer and selected hardwoods, 68" wide, 22" deep, 36" high, 1926. Part of a nine-piece set including a host chair, five side chairs, a table and a court cupboard.

Court cupboard (the name of a closed china cabinet) with four-piece V-matched mahogany veneer in middle panel, four piece diamond-matched mahogany veneer on side panels, butt mahogany veneer and drawer front and apron and selected hardwoods, 41" wide, 15" deep, 62" high, 1926. Part of a nine-piece set including a host chair, five side chairs, a table and a buffet.

When his father died, Will H. Gay headed the company. It was a progressive one, concerned with the welfare of the workman and was the first furniture producer to advertise on a national scale. This organization experimented with new methods and machinery, expanding until 1929 when the Simmons Company of Chicago purchased the company. In 1930, the poor economic conditions in the country caused the plant to close. Five years later the firm reopened under new management, did war work in World War II, but discontinued furniture production following the end of hostilities in 1945.

A nine-piece Berkey & Gay set consists of the three pieces pictured -- the host chair (always with arms), the buffet and a court cupboard, the name for an enclosed china cupboard. Five chairs and a table are not shown. Some companies permitted the purchaser to chose either a rectangular extension or a refectory (draw) table to complete a set.

During the Victorian Era of the 1800s, the decorating of furniture with carved flowers, figures, animals, roundels and other designs was extensive. When oak reigned for a few decades at the turn of the century, that form of ornamentation continued, but there was some change in motifs. Lions' paws formed feet. Griffins, imaginary creatures with an eagle head and wings and a lion's posterior; caryatids, a supporting pillar in the form of a woman; grotesque, the unnatural combination of human and animal parts; and other fantastic designs were present on elaborately decorated sideboards, desks, china cupboards and oversized hall trees.

Much of the craving for carvings departed when veneers replaced solid woods. It was the use of various types of veneer patterns that provided the decorations on furniture of the 1920s through the 1930s. The use of veneers for their beauty shows up well in the illustrations of several items from a ten-piece dining room set. The woods are listed under the pictures. In catalogues, many manufacturers itemized the actual veneers found on their furniture. For example, a quality set from 1927 combined mottled mahogany, striped mahogany and butt walnut veneers. In 1928 Oriental walnut, reversed diamond-matched zebrawood with madrone overlays and East Indian rosewood were combined on a case piece.

Buffet with straight-cut walnut veneer on top and sides, butt walnut veneer on doors and drawers, bird's-eye maple overlay panels on doors and selected hardwoods, 66" wide, 21" deep, 39" high, 1920s. Part of a ten-piece set including a host chair, five side chairs, a table, china cabinet and server.

Server with straight-cut walnut veneer on top and sides, butt walnut veneer on doors and apron, bird's-eye maple overlay panel on doors and selected hardwoods, 1920. Part of a ten-piece set including a host chair, five side chairs, a table, china cabinet and buffet.

China cabinet with straight-cut walnut veneer on top and sides, butt walnut veneer on drawer and side panels, bird's-eye maple overlay panel on drawer and selected hardwoods, 1920s. Part of a ten-piece set including a host chair, five side chairs, a table, server and buffet.

Side chair with modified shield back, V-matched mahogany veneer on splat and selected hardwoods, 40″ high, early 1930s. Part of a nine-piece set including five side chairs, a host chair, a table, china cabinet and buffet.

The Luce Furniture Company of Grand Rapids has roots that go back to a company formed in 1874, but the name Luce was not used until 1896. While the firm retained historical designs, in 1928 it devoted its principal efforts to Art Moderne furniture. For example, a dining room set included an extension table and case pieces with tops and ends of figured five-ply East Indian satinwood veneer. The buffet and cabinet drawer fronts were of English harewood with oval inlaid panels of satinwood, white holly and Macassar ebony banded with tulip wood. Despite the fact that a 1925 merger made the Luce Company one of the largest furniture manufacturers, it ceased operation in 1933 when much of the world experienced a depressed economy.

Some quality furniture factories were located at Louisville, Kentucky, and a nine-piece set marked with that city's name includes six chairs with modified shield backs that show the influence of the English cabinetmakers George Hepplewhite and Thomas Sheraton. Both the buffet and the china cabinet have a serpentine front portion. They also have inlay work in the form of flower baskets. The eclectic traits of the manufacturers can further be seen on the two doors of the china cabinet that resemble arches with dainty tracery reminiscent of Gothic church windows.

China cabinet with bird's-eye maple veneer, zebrawood veneer and marquetry on drawer front, zebrawood and marquetry on cabinet facing and selected hardwoods, 43″ wide, 17″ deep, 75″ high, 1930s. Part of a nine-piece set including a host chair, five side chairs, table and buffet.

Extension table with figured walnut veneer top, zebrawood veneer apron and selected hardwoods, 64" wide, 43" deep, 31" high, early 1930. Part of a nine-piece set including a host chair, five side chairs, china cabinet and buffet.

Side chair with mahogany veneer on back and selected hardwoods, 38" high, 1930s. Part of a six-piece set including a host chair, four side chairs, a table, buffet and china cabinet.

Buffet with figured walnut veneer top and sides, crotch walnut veneer outside door panels, maple veneer panels, bird's-eye veneer, zebrawood veneer and marquetry design on large drawer, zebrawood and marquetry on top drawer, and selected hardwoods, 78" wide, 25" deep, 39" high, 1930s. Part of a nine-piece set including a host chair, five side chairs, table and china cabinet.

When a family makes some sort of a record on a piece, it is helpful in determining its age. In pencil on the bottom of a chair it was noted that the upholstery was redone on April 7, 1941. The amount of material needed was also indicated - useful knowledge, indeed, for a new owner. In addition, if one assumes that the original fabric was retained for ten or more years before it was replaced, the chairs probably date to the 1930s or late 1920s. Such information, combined with a knowledge of what woods, styles and construction methods were utilized at a specified time helps determine the date of furniture.

China cabinet with plain-cut mahogany veneer on sides, drawer and door fronts and selected hardwoods, 37" wide, 15" deep, 74" high, 1930s. Part of a six-piece set including a host chair, five side chairs, a table and buffet.

Buffet with plain-cut mahogany veneer on top, sides, door and drawer fronts and selected hardwoods, 66″ wide, 21″ deep, 37″ high, 1930s. Part of a six-piece set including a host chair, five side chairs, a table and china cabinet.

Extension table with walnut veneer top, bleached V-matched striped walnut veneer on vertical support, butt walnut veneer oval overlay and selected hardwoods, 58″ wide, 42″ deep, 31″ high, late 1930s. Part of a four-piece set including a side chair, a host chair and buffet.

Blonde wood was advertised in the late 1930s and 1940s. As with human hair, it could be a natural or bleached. Walnut or mahogany were the customary dark woods that were artificially lightened. Nature's pale woods included birch, maple and light oak, but there were exotic species to consider as well. Avodire, holly, myrtle burl and satinwood were innately pale enough to pass as blondes.

Buffet with figured walnut veneer top and sides, V-matched Oriental veneer on bottom outside door and center panel, butt walnut veneer on two top drawers and outside of center drawers, maple veneer horizontal strips and veneerite (artificial) marquetry, 59″ wide, 20″ deep, 33″ high, late 1930s. Part of a four-piece set including a side chair, a host chair and a table.

As a generalization, it can be said that plain, straight lines were popular in the 1940s as characterized by the ribbed or channeled legs on

Host chair with bleached striped walnut veneer back and selected hardwoods, 23″ arm to arm, 42″ high, late 1930s. Part of a four-piece set including a side chair, extension table and buffet.

Dinette table made of selected hardwoods stained walnut, 43″ wide, 31″ deep, two 7″ leaves, 30″ high, early 1940s. Part of a six-piece dinette set including four side chairs and a buffet.

chairs and tables. Hardwoods stained walnut, veneers of walnut or mahogany or solid woods prevailed. The exotic veneers exited and furniture took on a calmer, less ornamental appearance.

Buffet made of selected hardwoods stained walnut, 41″ wide, 18″ deep, 35″ high, early 1940s. Part of a six-piece dinette set including four side chairs and a table.

A dining room set showing the buffet in the background, table with fold-up leaf, pin-striped walnut veneer top and selected hardwood base, 60″ wide, 42″ deep, 12″ leaf, 31″ high, and four chairs with V-matched pin-striped walnut veneer on back and selected hardwood bases, 34″ high, early 1940s.

Side chair made of selected hardwoods stained walnut, 30″ high, early 1940s. Part of a six-piece dinette set including four side chairs, a table and buffet.

Have you ever found the statement "Made in Grand Rapids" on a piece of furniture? It may or may not be authentic. For many years Grand Rapids, Michigan, was THE BIG NAME in the furniture industry. As early as 1908 "Made in Grand Rapids" labels were put on furniture not actually produced there. Aid was sought from the Federal Trade Commission, and offenders, including two companies from New Jersey, were forbidden use of the Grand Rapids name. Despite the gradual decline in the city's furniture leadership around the mid-1920s, many companies operated there. Because period styles were Grand Rapids' forte in the 1920s, various surviving factories continued to make traditional pieces, but they also attempted to remain competitive by manufacturing medium or low priced contemporary styles as well. Grand Rapids' gradual slip in its status can be seen by reading information from the *Furniture Dealers Reference Book* of 1928-1929 that names the fifteen leading household furnishing production centers as indicated in the following chart:

City	Number of Factories Supplying Products to Furniture Dealers in 1928 - 1929
Chicago	310
New York	280
Philadelphia	130
Grand Rapids	110
Brooklyn	68
Boston	61
Los Angeles	57
St. Louis	53
San Francisco	50
High Point, NC	49
Jamestown, NY	43
Cincinnati	38
Minneapolis	37
Rockford, IL	36
Cleveland	30

In many locations throughout Indiana there were furniture factories. The aforementioned reference book stated that Evansville, Indiana, alone had 36 factories that produced quality furniture in 1918 with an annual output of $25,000,000.

Information from the 1923-1924, 1928 and 1933 Montgomery Ward & Company catalogues and the Sears, Roebuck 1927 catalogue showed that the bulk of their bedroom and dining room furniture was shipped to customers directly from factories in Indiana. Indianapolis, Huntingburg, Richmond and Evansville were mentioned or geographical locations were indicated - central, southern and eastern Indiana - under the pictures of these sets.

A dining room set showing a Duncan Phyfe drop-leaf table with plain-cut walnut veneer top and selected hardwood base, 38″ wide, 26″ deep, 18″ drop leaves, 30″ high and five of six chairs made of selected hardwoods stained walnut, 30″ high, late 1940s.

Buffet with plain-cut mahogany veneer top and sides, crotch mahogany veneer drawer and door panels, 66″ wide, 22″ deep, 38″ high, 1920s, attributed to Flint & Horner Company, Inc., New York.

Buffet with high relief hunt scene on bottom drawer, book matched blistered oak on top drawer and oak burl veneer on the two doors, 66″ wide, 21″ deep, 39″ high, 1920s.

Buffet with mahogany veneer strips over V-matched maple veneer drawer, quilted maple veneer on doors with burl maple medallion in center, applied decorations, hand-painted designs and inlay patterns under drawer, 74″ wide, 21″ deep, 38″ high, 1930s.

Buffet with quarter-sliced English brown oak veneer on door panels, 68″ wide, 21″ deep, 36″ high, 1920s.

Buffet with figured Orientalwood top and sides, diamond-matched Orientalwood veneer and vertical zebranowood strips on drawer fronts, 48″ wide, 18″ deep, 35″ high, late 1930s.

Buffet with matched African mahogany veneer drawer and door fronts, 64" wide, 22" deep, 36" high, middle 1930s.

Photographs of china cabinets with traditional features appear in this chapter. For example, a broken pediment, a decorative top on furniture with a gap at the peak for an ornamental finial, crowns one example. Another is a breakfront china cabinet, one with three surfaces, the middle area projecting beyond the two end divisions to create a vertical break in the front of the piece. Because both of these styles attract customers, they remain popular.

In 1896, a mail-order company that bore his name was organized by Fred Macey, but after his death, its products were sold through retail stores. In 1916, the firm was purchased by R.W. Irwin, Earle S. Irwin and A.W. Hompe. It was owned by the Earle S. Irwin Company when World War II began and the factory was converted to war work by General Motors Corporation. Quality work was produced by the Robert W. Irwin Company, makers of attractive painted furniture. An Irwin cupboard decorated with bright floral bouquets is pictured.

China cabinet with applied decorations over walnut veneer panels and selected hardwood frame and base, 42" wide, 16" deep, 60" high, 1920s.

Modified-court cupboard made of plain-sliced figured maple with overlay veneer panels on doors and hand-painted designs, made by the Robert W. Irwin Company, Grand Rapids, 28" wide, 20" deep at base, 74" high, 1930s.

China cabinet with quarter-sliced tigerwood veneer facing panels and selected hardwood frame and base, 42" wide, 18" deep, 63" high, 1920s.

China cabinet with Macassar ebony two-tone veneer on side panels, bird's-eye maple overlay on drawer and selected hardwood base and frame, 37″ wide, 14″ deep, 69″ high, 1920s.

China cabinet with figured walnut veneer panels and drawer front, solid walnut back rail, three curly maple overlay designs and selected hardwood frame and base, 38″ wide, 14″ deep, 65″ high, 1920s.

China cabinet with walnut veneer door frame, side panels, drawer fronts and selected hardwood base, 40″ wide, 18″ deep, 69″ high, 1920s.

China cabinet with Oriental walnut veneer on cornice, drawer and doors and curly maple overlay above upper doors, on drawer and beneath lower doors, 36″ wide, 15″ deep, 68″ high, late 1930s.

China cabinet with crotch mahogany veneer on drawer and doors and convex glass on upper doors, 38" wide, 17" deep at base; 36" wide, 13" deep at top, 67" high, 1930s

Two-piece waterfall china cabinet with Oriental walnut veneer on top, sides and front and amber celluloid handles, 36" wide, 16" deep at base; 33" wide, 12" deep at top, 67" high, late 1930s.

Bow-front china cabinet with mahogany veneer sides, two-piece matching mahogany veneer drawer fronts and narrow banding above doors, made by Kling Factories, Mayville, New York, 35" wide, 17" deep, 71" high, 1930s.

China cabinet with mahogany veneer sides, door fronts and mahogany stained hardwood frame, 32" wide, 15" deep, 67" high, 1940s.

China cabinet with figured mahogany veneer sides and front facing, 45" wide, 15" deep, 82" high, 1940s.

Corner cupboard made of solid mahogany with crotch mahogany door and side panels, 32" wide, 18" deep, 71" high, 1930s.

Breakfront china cabinet with plain-cut walnut veneer on sides and walnut burl veneer front facing, 44" wide, 15" deep, 76" high, 1940s.

Corner cupboards have a following also, but they are fickle. They demand a place of their very own, free from obstructions so that they can be backed into a corner and stay there. It is well for a prospective buyer to measure in order to know that a location is available before the piece is purchased. Three such cupboards are pictured, one which has a rounded back, rather than the customary pointed type.

Corner cupboard with figured mahogany veneer pediment, door fronts and selected hardwood frame, 29" wide, 13" deep, 70" high, 1930s.

Corner cupboard with cherry veneer banding above upper doors and on fronts of drawer and doors, 36″ wide, 23″ deep, 71″ high, 1930s.

Since, as has already been stated, dining room sets were frequently offered by the piece, some people did not buy both the buffet and the server. The latter performed the same duties as the former, was smaller, cost less and was more convenient spacewise for a modest home. The same holds true today. A 1929 catalogue gave the server a dual purpose and a new dimension by stating, "Many people use it as a radio cabinet, with set on top and batteries inside."

Server with striped mahogany veneer on top, sides, door fronts, legs and stretcher, 42″ wide, 19″ deep, 33″ high, 1920s.

Server with plain-cut walnut veneer on top and sides and book match stumpwood walnut veneer on door fronts, 34″ wide, 18″ deep, 35″ high, 1920s.

Server with plain-cut walnut veneer top and ends and stump-wood walnut veneer on doors, 39″ wide, 19″ deep, 33″ high, 1920s.

Sheraton-style server with Australian maple butt veneer on drawers and apron and selected hardwood frame, 40″ wide, 20″ deep, 30″ high, 1930s.

Server with quarter-sliced paldao veneer side panels, mahogany veneer door panel with oval bird's-eye maple overlay and applied decorations, 36″ wide, 18″ deep, 34″ high, 1930s.

Occasionally, the label found on furniture is not that of the manufacturer. It can designate the store where the merchandise was sold. Such is the case with a serving table with drop ends that is pictured. Inside the middle divided drawer is a paper label with the name Lammert's, 10th & Washington, St. Louis. This was a wholesale and retail business started by Martin Lammert around 1861. Lammert noticed that areas in St. Louis where people shopped periodically declined in popularity as new sections developed. He declared he would never buy a building but would travel with the flow of the buying crowd. He did keep moving to bigger and better accommodations as his business grew. By 1910, as the shopping traffic moved westward, Lammert followed to 10th and Washington, and after his death, his son remained there until the expanding business necessitated a location change. In 1924, the company moved to 1911-1919 Washington Avenue. The label therefore tells one that the server was available to buyers sometime between 1910 and 1924. A brass tag inside the right drawer reads "Guaranteed solid mahogany." This information tells the buyer that it is solid mahogany except for the applied decorations.

Side chair with mahogany veneered splat, 43″ high, made by Rockford Furniture Company, 1920s.

Drop leaf serving table with a tag stating, "Guaranteed solid mahogany," distributed by Lammert's, 10th and Washington, St. Louis, 25″ wide, 18″ deep, 10″ drops, 30″ high, early 1920s.

Side chair made of selected hardwoods, 42″ high, 1920s; Art Moderne red and chrome smoker, 24″ high, made by Smoka-dore Manufacturing Company, Bloomfield, New Jersey, 1927.

Mahogany was popular and was in general use during the 1920s and 1930s. Frequently furniture fashioned from less expensive woods and stained to resemble it was labeled mahogany. This disturbed the Mahogany Association. In order to prevent confusion and misunderstandings, this group affixed plaques inside the drawers of approved pieces of furniture guaranteeing that all exterior surfaces were mahogany or mahogany veneer.

It was not unusual to assign dining room and kitchen chairs to other areas throughout the house. They served as companion pieces for desks or provided extra seats in living rooms, bedrooms or halls. Partly because of this need, chairs could be purchased individually rather than as a part of a set.

Currently, there tends to be a lack of formality in the serving of meals. This was not generally true of the 1920s, 1930s and 1940s when dining room furniture enhanced by fancy veneers had a special room of its own. The pictures included in this chapter attempt to show that dining rooms were an integral part of the American home during this era.

Desk chair with walnut veneer splat and walnut-stained selected hardwoods, pressed cane seat and French legs, 37" high, 1920s.

Gate-leg table with plain-cut walnut veneer top and walnut-stained selected hardwoods, 32" wide, 13" deep, 16" drop leaves, 1930s.

Side chair with four-piece matching burl walnut splat and walnut-stained selected hardwoods, 36" high, 1940s. This is one of a set of five chairs.

Gate-leg table made of selected hardwoods stained walnut, 24" wide, 11" deep, 14" drop leaves, 31" high, 1930s.

Chapter Five

Please Sit Down

Do you have a parlor as many houses did in the 19th century or is your comfortable area a living room? Years ago magazine editorials questioned why one room, a parlor, contained the best furniture and was saved for entertaining special guests. The family, the most important and most loved people in a home, should enjoy the finest surroundings available. Magazine feature articles challenged women to do away with the closed off parlor. So now - enter a living room and examine the furniture there.

Wing chair - that's a descriptive title for a design that once had a utilitarian purpose. It was a high back chair on which the back projected on each side in wings to shield the sitter from drafts. That term dates to the days when fireplaces provided heat and a person's posterior felt chilly while his front was toasty warm. When stoves brought more even heat, wings were frequently retained as a decorative feature. Early in the 1900s, chairs with pre-woven sheet cane on their seats and backs often were called wing chairs. This style persisted for decades and the two examples shown, a rocker and a pull-up chair, have mahogany stained hardwood frames.

Cane back and seat wing chair made of selected hardwoods finished dark; 25" arm to arm, 38" high, 1920s.

Cane back and seat wing rocker made of selected hardwoods finished dark, 23" arm to arm, 1920s.

Here's another term - overstuffed. That has a glutonous sound as if someone was as crammed full as a Thanksgiving foul. Actually, upholstered furniture from around 1897 to the 1930s bore this title. In the 1800s Victorians were expected to sit erect and, while some chairs of that era were comfortable, many were not. The generous paddings in the more modern living room sets allowed for slouching. Normally not much wood showed, but the portion that did was commonly a hardwood stained mahogany or walnut. Occasionally solid walnut was used. Frequently, an abbreviated wooden outline was seen on the front of the arms and meandered across the top of the back. A touch of carving added an attractive appearance to the frame. There was a mere suggestion of a leg. Many of the hardly perceptible feet on the chairs and davenports had a slight flair - a double curve - so they were dubbed Queen Anne.

Mohair upholstered arm chair with walnut frame and French legs, 28″ arm to arm, 33″ high, 1920s.

A tidy housewife attached antimacassars to the backs of her chairs. This name is derived from anti (against) plus macassar. The latter was a hair dressing shipped from a port of that name, spelled either with a 'k' or a 'c', in Indonesia. The purpose of the hand-crocheted backing was to protect the chair from head oil soil. The arms were covered with smaller versions.

Loose cushions on the seats were favored and tended to be reversible so that a different pattern or fabric was exposed by flipping the cushions. This had two advantages. It changed the appearance and helped equalize wear. A set, still in the possession of its original owners, is shown and retains its 1928 upholstered fabrics with floral velour on one side and a tapestry, depicting baskets of flowers, on the other.

Wing chair with original upholstery, velour sides and carved hardwood frame, 34″ arm to arm, 38″ high, 1928. Part of a two-piece set including davenport.

Arm chair upholstered in red velvet with carved hardwood frame, 31″ arm to arm, 39″ high, late 1920s.

Davenport with original upholstery, reversible seats with tapestry baskets on one side of cushions and floral velour on the other and a carved hardwood frame, 78″ wide, 34″ high, 1928. Part of a two-piece set including wing chair.

Upholstered davenport with carved hardwood frame, 77″ arm to arm, 38″ high, 1930s. Part of a two-piece set.

Upholstered arm chair with carved hardwood frame, 31" arm to arm, 38" high, 1930s. Part of a two-piece set including davenport.

An illustrated three-piece set, that the manufacturer called a Queen Anne suite, consists of a lady's chair and a davenport upholstered in matching rose brocade. The gentleman's wing chair has a tapestry covering with rose highlights.

Arm chair with brocade upholstery, carved crest and carved hardwood frame, 36" arm to arm, 36" high, 1930s. Part of three-piece set including wing chair and davenport.

Identifying names have been given to certain chairs and davenports. Although details such as legs, cushion treatment and trims vary widely, the general shape retains a familial similarity. Types that remain popular through the years are included in the production lines of many manufacturers. Shell, open arm pull-up and barrel are some of the continuing named shapes for chairs. To add a classical note, the Empire Chair Company, Johnson City, Tennessee, offered chairs in two popular period styles - Tudor and Jacobean.

Wing chair with tapestry upholstery, carved crest and carved hardwood frame, 36" arm to arm, 40" high, 1930s. Part of three-piece set including arm chair and davenport.

Upholstered shell (or easy) chair with carved designs on hardwood frame, 32" arm to arm, 35" high, 1930s.

Davenport with brocade upholstery, carved crest and carved hardwood frame, 83" arm to arm, 36" high, 1930s. Part of three-piece set including wing chair and davenport.

On floors, Oriental style rugs were prevalent during the first half of the 1900s, and these patterns consistently retain their popular status.

At times davenports were advertised with the addition of a qualifying statement that they were available as bed davenports also. Even more specific was the description that a long or short version could be purchased. The sleeper portion pulled out parallel to the seat when the davenport was a long one. On the short styles the sleeping section extended out from the seat.

The Kroehler Company of Naperville, Illinois, began operating in 1893, and one of their long sleepers is pictured. Conveniently, it can be used to sleep two, or it can be separated to form twin beds. It still wears its original mohair covering, a popular fabric in the late 1930s and early 1940s, but because it pricks, it is disliked by children.

In addition to the already mentioned velour, tapestry, brocade and mohair, damask, plush, velvet and leather - both real and imitation - were upholstery fabrics. That overstuffed look represented comfort, and the coverings chosen helped create a cozy, colorful decor.

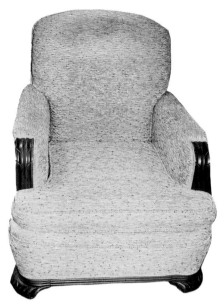

Upholstered arm chair with rolled and ribbed designed hardwood arms and feet, 31″ arm to arm, 34″ high, 1935. Part of two-piece set including davenport that is not pictured.

Arm chair with original mohair upholstery made by Kroehler, 35″ arm to arm, 33″ high, 1930s. Part of two-piece set including davenport bed.

Davenport bed with original mohair upholstery made by Kroehler, late 1930s. Part of two-piece set including arm chair.

Barrel chair with tufted back, French legs and mahogany-finished hardwood frame, 26″ arm to arm, 35″ high, 1940s.

Chapter Six

The Bedroom

She's a hussy! That was a contemptuous phrase frequently assigned to a woman of questionable morality. One quick way a pre-1900 female in the United States earned this title was to use cosmetics. A concept of sin seemed to be associated with make-up when this nation was caught up in its Victorian Era standards of conduct. Following World War I, many women dared to abbreviate both their floor length dresses and long tresses and they could vote. Some entered the business world. Such women were not afraid to try to improve their appearances by adding color to their faces. Magazine articles encouraged the practice and denied it was evil.

Manufacturers, always on the quest for new trends, realized that women who use make-up needed a place to primp. They designed a boudoir piece for them and the resulting toilet (dressing) table became a focal point in the bedroom. At that time, the word toilet referred to personal grooming. This meaning continues currently since toiletries include soaps, lotions, colognes or perfumed toilet water for the skin or bath. A dressing table set incorporated a bench or chair so that a lady sat as she primped - brushing, combing and applying lipstick, powder and rouge. Soon the name was changed to vanity dressers or semi-vanities. The latter had fewer drawers. Because Hollywood was the world's movie center, some companies called their dressing tables

Dressing table with plain-cut walnut veneer top and edges, figured walnut veneer drawer front, selected hardwood frame and applied decorations on drawer front, stiles and apron, 34" wide, 18" deep, 57" high, early 1920s made by Forsyth Furniture Company, Winston-Salem, North Carolina. Part of a two-piece set including dresser.

Dresser with plain-cut walnut veneer top and sides, figured walnut veneer drawer fronts, selected hardwood frame and applied decorations on drawer front, stiles, back rail and mirror frame, 42" wide, 21" deep, 70" high, early 1920s made by Forsyth Furniture Company, Winston-Salem, North Carolina. Part of a two-piece set including dressing table.

"Hollywood" vanities in order to associate them with the glamorous movie stars.

Triple mirrors were popular. The middle plate was longer and wider than the pivoting side ones that could be adjusted to enable a woman to see her profile, full face or the back of her head. These looking glasses had continuous wooden frames.

Men too had furniture designed for them. The new type storage units, called chifforettes, came in various sizes and styles and usually stood on legs. They frequently had a long drawer at the base with two doors above. When the latter was opened, sliding trays with sides were exposed in which a man's folded shirts, detachable stiffly starched white collars or other personal possessions were easily accessible.

Chifforobes stood tall and generally had two doors. On one side a sliding pull-out feature held hangers for garments. There were trays or drawers for storage behind the other door. For a slight charge a full-length mirror was added to the front of one or both doors.

Chifforette with burl walnut, burl mahogany, bird's-eye maple and Macassar ebony veneers on drawer and door fronts, 40″ wide, 20″ deep, 59″ high, 1929, made by the Table Rock Furniture Company, Morgantown, North Carolina. Part of a three-piece set including dresser and bed.

Poster bed with burl mahogany veneer on headboard and burl mahogany and bird's-eye maple veneer on footboard, 1929, made by the Table Rock Furniture Company, Morgantown, North Carolina. Part of a three-piece set including dresser and chifforette.

Dresser with plain-cut mahogany veneer top and sides, burl mahogany veneer on two large drawers and beeswing mahogany and zebrawood veneers on top drawers, 50″ wide, 23″ deep, 71″ high, 1929. Part of a three-piece set including bed and chifforette.

A chiffonier, a tall chest of drawers, was usually a male's piece. The trend was toward a leggy look and pieces stood on turned legs. Manufacturers eulogized the dustproof construction on the case pieces in which each drawer was separated from the one above and below by a dustproof partition. Center guides on drawers helped them move in and out easily and replaced the two slides, one on each side, formerly used. Any type of a dome or cathedral top was considered elite and this small arched compartment incorporated a series of little drawers behind a door.

Dressing table with plain-cut walnut veneer top and sides, burl walnut veneer drawer front, curly maple veneer panels under two outside mirrors and oak cornice and panel under drawer, 51″ wide, 19″ deep, 75″ high, early 1920s. Part of a four-piece set including poster bed, dresser and bench.

Poster bed with burl walnut veneer on headboard and footboard panels, oak cornice on headboard and oak panel on foot board, 56″ high head posts, 46″ high foot posts, early 1920s. Part of a four-piece set including dresser, dressing table and bench.

Dressing table bench made of selected hardwoods finished to match set, 27″ wide, 14″ deep, 22″ high, early 1920s. Part of a four-piece set including poster bed, dresser and dressing table.

Dresser with plain-cut walnut veneer top and sides, burl walnut veneer drawer front, curly maple veneer panels under two outside mirrors and oak top cornice, 52″ wide, 22″ deep, 76″ high, early 1920s. Part of a four-piece set including poster bed, dressing table and bench.

Pictured in Chapter Two is a bow end bed, with rounded foot boards and six legs, that was in style until the late 1920s. Poster types with tall, turned posts at each corner were popular in the 1920s and 1930s. Straight end beds with panels were in vogue in the 1930s. On one of the four-piece bedroom sets shown, the name Sligh is stenciled on the back of the bed headboard and a paper label inside the drawer of the chiffonier says Sligh Furniture, Grand Rapids. A vanity and bench complete the walnut veneer set with its cheerfully painted floral designs.

It was in 1880, that Charles R. Sligh, Sr. started the Sligh Furniture Company with L.H. Randall as its president. This factory specialized in bedroom furniture and became one of Grand Rapids' largest firms with 850 employees in 1920. The plant closed in 1931, four years after the death of its founder. His namesake son helped establish a new firm, the

Charles R. Sligh Company, at Holland, Michigan, in 1933 where general furnishings for the home were produced. The Sligh-Lowry Furniture Company originated when a plant that produced household desks and bookcases was acquired in Zeeland, Michigan, in 1940. In 1945 Sligh-Lowry purchased the Grand Rapids Chair Company that manufactured chairs when it was first established, but by the 1880s added bedroom and dining room furniture to its lines. This plant was sold in 1957.

Bed with four-piece matched butt walnut veneer on head and footboard panels, striped mahogany raised veneer panel on footboard and curly maple veneer panels on which floral designs have been hand-painted, 57″ wide, 48 high at head, 30″ high at foot, 1920s, made by Sligh Furniture Company, Grand Rapids. Part of a four-piece set including chiffonier, vanity table and bench.

Vanity table with plain-cut walnut veneer top and sides, butt walnut veneer on two side drawers, curly maple veneer on center drawer onto which floral designs have been hand-painted and zebranowood veneer strips above and below the drawers, 46″ wide, 19″ deep, 60″ high; bench is made of selected hardwoods finished walnut with a pressed cane seat, 30″ wide, 15″ deep, 17″ high, 1920s, made by the Sligh Furniture Company, Grand Rapids. Part of a four-piece set including bed, chiffonier and bench.

It is a complex task to follow the history of companies as ownerships changed or unions with other firms occurred. Oftentimes large organizations emerged as a result of mergers.

A decorative effect common to the late 1920s resulted when a light toned veneer was placed over dark woods such as walnut and mahogany to create a contrast. Maple was a frequent selection for such overlays and its varied patterns were given descriptive names such as tiger, bird's-eye or curly.

Chiffonier with plain-cut walnut veneer top and sides, butt walnut veneer on three bottom drawers and outer parts of top drawer and curly maple veneer panel in center of top drawer onto which floral designs have been hand-painted, 36″ wide, 20″ deep, 47″ high, 1920s, made by Sligh Furniture Company, Grand Rapids. Part of a four-piece set including bed, vanity table and bench.

Bed with curly maple veneer panel flanked by striped mahogany veneer on headboard, 58″ wide, 56″ high headboard, 30″ high footboard, late 1920s. Part of a four-piece set including chest of drawers, vanity and bench.

Chest of drawers with curly maple veneer panel, striped mahogany veneer on drawers, router lines and applied decorations, 38" wide, 20" deep, 51" high, late 1920s. Part of a four-piece set including bed, vanity and bench.

If a person's pocketbook and rooms were both small, it was possible to purchase items for the bedroom individually. Only a bed and chiffonier were essential. If a family bought a three-piece set consisting of a bed (panel, poster or twin), choice of a dresser or vanity and a chest of drawers, it was customary to receive a reduced price for the grouping. Additional pieces included a chifforobe, chifforette, rocker and a chair. When an item of furniture designed for hanging clothes had one door in the center, some manufacturers referred to it as closette. As opposed to a chifforobe, it did not provide drawer space.

A one-door wardrobe helped when a family lacked closets. For a few additional dollars, it was possible to have chifforobes, chifforettes and wardrobes cedar-lined as a protection against moth damage.

Vanity with plain-cut mahogany veneer top and sides, striped mahogany, bird's-eye maple and curly maple veneers on mirror frame, drawers and apron, 46" wide, 18" deep, 70" high; bench is made of selected hardwoods finished to match set, 20" wide, 16" deep, 22" high, late 1920. Part of a five-piece set including bed (not pictured), dresser and closette.

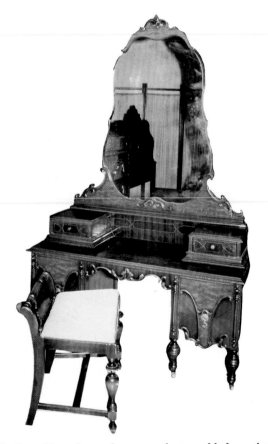

Vanity with curly maple veneer above and below mirror and above bottom drawers, striped mahogany veneer between boxes and on drawer fronts, 48" wide, 18" deep, 73" high, late 1920s. Part of a four-piece set including bed, chest of drawers and bench.

Dresser with plain-cut mahogany veneer top and sides, striped mahogany, bird's-eye maple and curly maple veneers on mirror frame, drawers and apron and a selected hardwood frame, 44″ wide, 20″ deep, 71″ high, late 1920s. Part of a five-piece set including bed (not pictured), vanity, bench and closette.

Cedar-lined wardrobe with V-matched Oriental walnut veneer on door and figured Oriental walnut veneer on the rest of the case, 24″ wide, 21″ deep, 65″ high, late 1930s.

Waterfall, a fanciful name for the front of furniture from the mid-1930s, denotes a pronounced roll instead of a flat, sharp edge on the top surface. This round effect was present on the chest of drawers, the dresser, the vanity and the head and footboard. When this fashion was inaugurated, a large round mirror often without a frame, was characteristically included on vanities. The glass gradually diminished in size and assumed a rectangular shape in the 1940s. A vanity with a drop center, often displayed in fashionable homes of the 1940s, was one where the middle section was lower than its flanking drawers or doors.

Closette (wardrobe) with striped mahogany, bird's-eye maple and curly maple veneers on door, drawer and panels, 38″ wide, 20″ deep, 70″ high, late 1920s. Part of a five-piece set including bed (not pictured), dresser, vanity and bench.

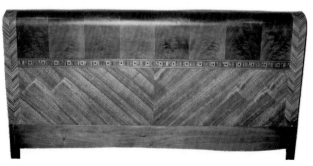

Bed headboard with V-matched zebranowood and butt walnut veneer panels, 56″ wide, 44″ high, late 1930s. Part of a three-piece waterfall set including chest of drawers and vanity.

Bed with matched and V-matched Oriental walnut veneer separated by zebrawood and mahogany banding, 57" wide, 41" high headboard, 23" high footboard, late 1930s. Part of the following five-piece waterfall set including dresser, vanity, bench (not pictured) and chifforobe.

Vanity with Oriental walnut veneer on top, sides and center drawer front and diamond-matched and two-tone V-matched zebranowood on the rest of the case, 50" wide, 18" deep, 65" high, 44" diameter mirror, late 1930s. Part of a three-piece waterfall set including bed and chest of drawers.

Dresser with matched Oriental walnut veneer on top and sides, diamond and V-matched Oriental walnut veneer on drawers and a banding of zebranowood and marquetry separating the first two drawers, 44" wide, 20" deep, 71" high, late 1930s. Part of the five-piece waterfall set.

Chest of drawers with Oriental walnut veneer on top and sides, crotch claro (walnut) veneer on top drawers, two-tone diamond-matched zebranowood on bottom drawers, and V-matched zebranowood on stiles, late 1930s. Part of a three-piece waterfall set including bed and vanity.

Vanity with matched Oriental walnut veneer on top and sides, diamond and V-matched Oriental walnut veneer on drawers and a banding of zebranowood and marquetry above apron, 44" wide, 18" deep, 66" high, 1930s. Part of the five-piece waterfall set.

Bed with diamond and V-matched zebranowood panels, 41″ high headboard, 24″ high footboard, 1930s. Part of a two-piece waterfall set including dresser made by D. Bassett Manufacturing Company, (Bedroom Furniture) Bassett, Virginia.

Chifforobe with matched Oriental walnut veneer on top and sides, diamond and V-matched Oriental walnut veneer on door and drawers and a banding of zebranowood and marquetry separating the first two drawers; the cabinet behind the door is cedar-lined, 36″ wide, 20″ deep, 62″ high, late 1930s. Part of the five-piece waterfall set including bed, dresser, vanity and bench (not pictured).

In the late 1920s and through the 1930s, zebrawood or zebrano frequently was used as a decorative veneer in combination with walnut or Orientalwood, also known as Australian walnut. Inlay strips and celluloid drawer pulls added allure. On some less expensive pieces, veneerite, a thin paperlike material, was applied to emulate expensive veneers.

Many companies produced artistically decorated furniture in the 1930s. Decal transfers or stencils were used by some manufacturers, but others employed skilled artists to execute designs. The results were both cheerful and expensive. One company's efforts are present in a four-piece set consisting of twin beds, a chest of drawers and a console chest with three drawers in the center and two

Dresser with quarter-sliced avodire on top and sides, diamond and V-matched zebranowood veneer on outside doors and mirror frame and satinwood veneer overlay panels beneath mirror and on middle drawer, 46″ wide, 18″ deep, 71″ high, 1930s. Part of a two-piece waterfall set including bed made by D. Bassett Manufacturing Company, (Bedroom Furniture) Bassett, Virginia.

Twin bed with plain-cut mahogany veneer, cupids in oval panels, urn on top rail of headboard and hand-painted designs, 41″ wide, 45″ high at head, 26″ high at foot, 1930s. Part of a four-piece set including twin beds, chest of drawers and console, made by Johnson Furniture Company, Grand Rapids, Michigan.

rounded doors at each side. On the top surface two doors open to reveal three drawers. Inside one is a treasure or trinket tray that slides forward and back. Additional drawer space is at the base.

A brass plaque, marked Johnson Furniture Company, Grand Rapids, Michigan, is found inside the top drawer of the console chest, one part of a three-piece bedroom set pictured here. Johnson was a company that did not restrict itself to bedroom pieces but produced a general line of household furnishings. When inside details are as well executed as the outer designs, it is a sign of concerned workmanship. This set qualifies for this distinction. Such quality painted pieces as these were often more costly than veneered examples.

Chest of drawers with plain-cut mahogany veneer, cupids, an urn and hand-painted designs with three drawers behind the top doors, 38″ wide, 21″ deep, 60″ high, 1930s. Part of a four-piece set including twin beds and a console, made by Johnson Furniture Company, Grand Rapids, Michigan.

Console with plain-cut mahogany veneer, cupids, an urn and hand painted design, 49″ wide, 23″ deep, 36″ high, 1930s. Part of a four-piece set including twin beds and a chest of drawers, made by Johnson Furniture Company, Grand Rapids, Michigan.

A unique way to name a furniture company was to honor its founding date. Two men with imagination did that. D.S. Brown and J.C. Rickenbaugh formed a partnership in 1900 as a new century began, and they decided to call their firm Century Furniture Company. It was located in Grand Rapids, widely known for its high quality reproductions of classical styles, and was eventually one of the city's leading manufacturers.

In a 1928 pamphlet distributed to celebrate Grand Rapids' one hundredth furniture market, Century Company stated that they desired to authentically interpret the arts and craftsmanship of preceding furniture periods. To recreate furniture properly, historical research, coupled with intelligence and imagination was necessary. Only with this essential background was it possible to secure the rare woods and devote the extensive time required to create their copies authentically.

An exhibit at the Grand Rapids Museum shows products purchased in the 1930s from the Century factory showroom. All are copies of masterpieces or original creations based on historic, classical motifs. The colorful display borrowed designs from the craftsmen of Egypt, Rome, England, Spain and France. Inspiration was derived from inspecting the works of Duncan Phyfe, by studying early American themes, and by examining modern designs. Many of the pieces were painted, some with Chinese design. Gracefully curved legs, gilted surfaces and fancy inlay work yielded a French feel. All were ornately and beautifully wrought. There are fine examples of quality painted pieces included in this book, but unfortunately, none is identified by a Century label. This company ceased to exist with a separate identity after its purchase by Murray Furniture Company in 1940.

The 1930s was a decade of experimentation. The Art Moderne school developed metal furniture and frequently artificially grained it to give it the look of wood. Streamlining, especially in industry, was the effect the American designer Norman Bel Geddes promoted and he was perhaps its leading advocate. Examine the pictures of a single bed, a dresser and a four-drawer chest. This metal set is similar to one displayed in the department store windows of Carson, Pirie Scott while the Century of Progress Expositon was attracting thousands of visitors to Chicago in 1934.

The latter set was designed by Norman Bell Geddes for the Simmons Company, New York, New York. In 1935, this firm was advertised as the world's largest maker of furniture and bedding. Their wares included davenports that folded out into beds that were either double or twin units. While the Geddes display set was black lacquer and chrome, the one illustrated in this book is yellow with chrome trim. For the 1939 and 1940 New York World's Fair, Geddes looked ahead 20 years and created Futurama, a replica of a city-to-come in 1960. He envisioned streamlined autos rushing along on multi-level highways amid towering skyscrapers. History shows that Geddes was an accurate prophet.

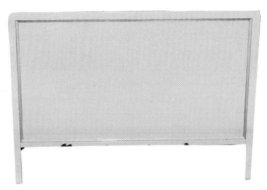

Headboard of single metal bed similar to a black metal bed that was a part of a set seen in a display window in Chicago's Carson Pirie Scott during the second year of the Century of Progress, 1934. Part of the following three-piece metal set made by Simmons and possibly designed by Norman Bel Geddes.

Art Moderne metal dressing table with artificial wood graining, 48" wide, 17" deep, 70" high and matching bench, 21" wide, 14" deep, 17" high, 1930s. Part of a four-piece set including a bed (not pictured) and chest of drawers. This set is attributed to Norman Bel Geddes, a leading designer of the period.

Dresser similiar to black metal dresser that was a part of a set seen in a display window in Chicago's Carson Pirie Scott during the second year of the Century of Progress, 1934. Dresser size is 39" wide, 19" deep, 35" high. Part of the three-piece metal set.

Art Moderne metal chest of drawers with artificial wood graining, 34" wide, 19" deep, 45" high, 1930s. Part of a four-piece set including a bed (not pictured), dressing table and bench. This set is attributed to Norman Bel Geddes, a leading designer of the period.

Chest of drawers similiar to black metal chest that was a part of a set seen in a display window in Chicago's Carson Pirie Scott during the second year of the Century of Progress, 1934. Chest size is 31" wide, 19" deep, 45" high. Part of the metal set including single bed and dresser made by Simmons and possibly designed by Norman Bel Geddes.

Other exponents of Art Moderne furniture were two outstanding American architects, Frank Lloyd Wright and Eliel Saarinen, both of whom advocated a geometric approach to furniture designs. Because Wright felt furniture should harmonize with its setting, he created modernistic furniture for the homes he built. The majority of it is now in the possession of collectors or in museums.

Paul T. Frankl considered the American skyscraper a vital contribution to modern art. He created skyscraper furniture.

In 1932, Donald Deskey's interior of Radio City Music Hall in New York City's Rockefeller Center stressed the Art Moderne look. Furniture of chrome plated steel and tube aluminum was in evidence. Gilbert Rohde, also a furniture designer, made tubular tables.

An unusual Art Moderne three-piece bedroom set of wood painted black with silver lines was made by the Rockford Furniture Manufacturing Company, Rockford, Illinois. Only the headboard of the bed is pictured, but the footboard has the same pattern. All the drawers in the set have center slides and dust partitions between the drawers. A small removable mirror on the dresser has a black and silver frame. The all-in-one-unit vanity with its tall frameless mirror and its stool with a spin-around top is unique. A shaving stand, a separate piece but not a part of the set, seen on top of the chest portion can be folded down to form a box. Its color, however, matches the set. Can you imagine a bosomless, low waisted young flapper's reaction to this bedroom outfit? As she slouched along, swinging her long strand of beads, she'd probably stop and purr with pleasure, "Look at this vanity. It's the cat's meow!"

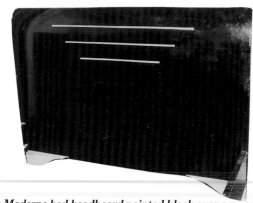

Art Moderne bed headboard painted black over a wooden base 57″ wide, 41″ high headboard, 23″ high footboard, late 1930s. Part of a four-piece set including a dresser, vanity and stool made by Rockford Furniture Manufacturing Company, Rockford, Illinois.

Art Moderne vanity painted black over a wooden base with chrome plated drawer pulls, 18″ wide, 19″ deep; mirror, 22″ wide, 68″ high and stool, 16″ diameter, 18″ high, late 1930s. Part of a four-piece set including bed and chest of drawers made by Rockford Furniture Manufacturing Company, Rockford, Illinois.

Art Moderne chest of drawers painted black over a wooden base with a portable mirror and chrome plated drawer pulls, 36″ wide, 19″ deep, 49″ high, late 1930s. Part of a four-piece set including a bed, vanity and stool made by Rockford Furniture Manufacturing Company, Rockford, Illinois.

Other styles were available and appealed to more conventional families. Frequently, poster bedroom sets of the 1920s and the 1930s were painted "old ivory". Swags, baskets of flowers and incised lines provided decorations. A set shown includes a chifforette with a difference because its drawers are cedar-lined to discourage moths. The manufacturer was identified as The Helmers Manufacturing Company, Wholesale Furniture, Kansas City, Missouri, USA and Leavenworth Factory, Leavenworth, Kansas, USA.

Poster bed with old ivory finish, incised decorative lines and applied decorations, 56″ wide, 56″ high headboard, 52″ high footposts, late 1930s. Part of a three-piece set including a chifforette and a dressing table made by the Helmers Manufacturing Company, Leavenworth, Kansas.

Chifforette with old ivory finish, incised decorative lines and applied decorations; there are three pull-out drawers behind the two doors, 34″ wide, 20″ deep, 49″ high, late 1930s. Part of a three-piece set including a poster bed and dressing table made by the Helmers Manufacturing Company, Leavenworth, Kansas.

As the 1940s commenced, it seemed that a full circle was completed in regard to the wood used during the 1920s through the 1940s. In the early 1920s, walnut and mahogany were the most common woods. In the 1940s, again there was a swing to these two species and other more subdued veneers in contrast to the look furniture manufacturers promoted from the late 1920s through the 1930s when varieties of exotic woods were mixed and matched in order to obtain unusual decorative effects and patterns.

Dressing table with old ivory finish, incised decorative lines and applied decorations, 48″ wide, 18″ deep, 71″ high, late 1930s. Part of a three-piece set including a poster bed and chifforette made by the Helmers Manufacturing Company, Leavenworth, Kansas.

Bed made of solid walnut, 57″ wide, 36″ high headboard, 26″ high footboard, 1940s. Part of a four-piece set including chest-on-chest, vanity dresser and vanity stool.

Vanity stool made of solid walnut with French legs and applied shell on knees, 22″ wide, 16″ deep, 18″ high, 1940s. Part of a four-piece set including bed, chest-on-chest and vanity dresser.

Chest-on-chest made of solid walnut, 36″ wide, 20″ deep, 51″ high, 1940s. Part of a four-piece set including bed, vanity dresser and vanity stool.

Bed made of selected hardwoods finished walnut, 56″ wide, 36″ high headboard, 22″ high footboard, 1946. Part of a four-piece set including chest of drawers, vanity and vanity bench made by Kroehler.

Vanity dresser made of solid walnut with attached mirror, 48″ wide, 20″ deep, 31″ to top of vanity; mirror, 25″ wide, 38″ high, 1940s. Part of a four-piece set including bed, chest-on-chest and vanity stool.

Vanity bench made of selected hardwoods finished walnut, 21″ wide, 13″ deep, 18″ high, 1946. Part of a four-piece set including bed, chest of drawers and vanity made by Kroehler.

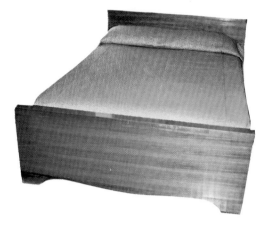

Bed with walnut veneer, 57″ wide, 32″ high headboard, 21″ high footboard, 1945. Part of a three-piece set including dresser and chest of drawers.

Vanity made of selected hardwoods finished walnut, 46″ wide, 18″ deep, 62″ high, 1946. Part of a four-piece set including bed, chest of drawers and vanity bench made by Kroehler.

Dresser with walnut veneer and handleless drawer fronts, 44″ wide, 19″ deep, 66″ high, 1945. Part of a three-piece set including bed and chest of drawers.

Chest of drawers made of selected hardwoods finished walnut, 34″ wide, 20″ deep, 49″ high, 1946. Part of a four-piece set including bed, vanity and vanity bench made by Kroehler.

Chest of drawers with walnut veneer and handleless drawer fronts, 32″ wide, 18″ deep, 49″ high, 1945. Part of a three-piece set including bed and dresser.

In late 1939 much of Europe was embroiled in battles and bombings, and it did not seem important to risk shipping cargoes of imported woods across the ocean to North America. Following the entry of the United States into the war in December, 1941, when factories were converted to meet the nation's military needs, there were shortages of many raw materials. It was difficult, for example, to secure walnut for furniture use because it was needed for gun stocks.

Evansville, Indiana, was well known for its production of quality furniture. In June, 1944, slightly over a year before the war ended, Evansville's Imperial Desk Company advised their customers via letters that, due to the restrictions placed under Limitation Order No. 260-A, they could not, after July 1, offer more than 25% of the patterns that were active as of September, 1941. Various articles were then listed with the addendum that "All other items . . . other than those specifically referred to have been temporarily suspended from production until victory."

The Chittenden-Eastman Company of Burlington, Iowa, expressed its wartime message as follows: "Owing to present conditions many materials may become unavailable. We, therefore, reserve the right to change our specification without notice." This warning was expressed several times in their 1942-43 catalogue.

It is enlightening to read the descriptions of some of the bedroom furniture that was produced in the 1920s, 1930s and 1940s. As the 1920s began, mahogany and walnut, as previously stated, were the prominent veneers used.

However by the mid-1920s, more veneers were putting in their appearance, including butt walnut, rosewood, tulipwood and figured or bird's-eye maple overlays, often combined with gold or ebony line decorations. Mottled mahogany and half-diamond figured mahogany as well as blistered maple created elaborate drawer fronts or panels. Drawers on some chests bore gilded carving, hand-painted polychrome shading or stippled borders. Hand-painted floral decorations added color.

Near the end of this decade, painted sets were available and a shaded green arcadian enamel over walnut and gum was a popular hue. Red and gray touches or decalcomania decorations were attractive. It seems as if an attempt to glamorize furniture by highlighting it with various patterns of veneers inspired designers to seek exotic woods. African, Oriental and moire walnut, reversed diamond-matched zebrawood with madrone overlays, East Indian rosewood, blistered maple veneers, avodire, Macassar ebony and Carpathian elm were mentioned in 1929 furniture catalogues. It appeared that a race was on to determine which company could find the rarest woods and employ the most complicated veneers to enhance its products.

Some of the veneers that were prevalent in the 1930s included: curly birch, cherry, burl laurel, bird's-eye maple, tigerwood, laurel, Orientalwood, butt walnut, madrone burl, quarter sawed curly American ash, V-matched striped walnut, V-matched zebrawood, basket weave zebrawood, African walnut, burl Italian olive wood, swirl oak, crotch mahogany, Brazilian rosewood and Carpathian elm burl. Imagine what striking effects were possible when these veneers were combined to form various patterns. The results were frequently as dramatic as the woods themselves.

In the mid-1930s, Circassian walnut fronts with salixwood (black willow) tops were available. The less expensive sets had imitation curly maple decorations while those of medium quality had rotary-sawed walnut tops, fronts and ends. Quilted poplar drawer fronts and bird's-eye maple overlays were present. Some sets had router lines with black stencil and imitation lacewood decorations. In the center of drawers, a curly maple sunburst design frequently sent forth its rays. Orientalwood tops with V-matched fronts enticed buyers. Stump Australian maple gave eye catching appeal to quality sets. On another expensive set, the top and ends were of blistered maple with a vivid burl acacia wood front. High quality examples listed satinwood tops and ends, crotch aspen fronts with satinwood borders. Others had the satinwood tops, fronts and ends with kao wood front panels and tulipwood banding at the base. Tigerwood tops and ends and a combination of tigerwood and sliced walnut formed fronts. Prima vera and aspen were other veneers.

Some companies advertised Art Moderne styles. Featured were ribbed designs, and salixwood or sliced walnut tops with chromium or onyx (sometimes called marblene onyx) hardware. Metal handles with celluloid center were prevalent also. Orientalwood fronts and V-matching in contrasting directions were common. Footboards of beds might have three panels with lines going up and down, horizontally and V-shaped. Ivory and black router lines were used in stippled decorations.

The late 1930s legless case pieces tended to be straight and squared in their lines with metal drawer handles. Diamond-matched fronts of striped walnut were popular and tops of sliced or butt walnut or of marowood were used. Zebrawood, colobra (kelobra), Carpathian elm, V-matched African walnut or Orientalwood created figured fronts. Rosewood decorated drawers. Frequently, it was more convenient for a manufacturer to say five-ply fancy wood tops and not to specify the veneers precisely. Large round mirrors appeared on dressers or were placed on the wall above them. The waterfall style brought a roll to the top of bedroom pieces.

Drop center vanities with the middle lower than the sides were prevalent. Sets comprised of four-way matched butt or striped walnut, New Guinea wood, prima vera or fiddleback mahogany were shown. These veneers appeared in different combinations.

It was hard to buy furniture in 1945 following the termination of World War II when the military personnel were returning and establishing homes. Many newlyweds bought from second-hand shops since they could not wait for factories to return to peacetime schedules. Others raided family attics and basements for castoffs. This shortage influenced the decors of those years.

A waterfall vanity, pictured here, has an electric light inset under the mirror. The edge of the glass is encircled by etching. Another pictured version with a large round mirror has a drop center. Clothes of the depression vintage are reflected in the glass. Sometimes benches or chairs become separated from the vanities. A group of these stray seats is illustrated. As can be seen, most of them have ribbed legs, a style that developed late in the 1930s, and was dominant in the 1940s.

Vanity with quarter-sliced zebrawood veneer tops, sides, drawer fronts and banding framing drawers, with clothes of the period showing in mirror, 46″ wide, 18″ deep, 66″ high; mirror 42″ diameter, middle 1930s.

Some chifforettes and chifforobes show serpentine (waving in and out) or projection fronts where the top drawer extends over the ones below. These features helped individualize chests and dressers.

Vanity with matched and V-matched quarter-sliced Oriental wood veneer on tops, sides, drawer fronts and zebrawood horizontal and vertical banding around drawers and mirror frame, 50″ wide, 18″ deep, 65″ high, late 1930s.

Chifforette with striped mahogany veneer on top, sides and drawer and door fronts; pull-out drawers behind the doors, 38″ wide, 20″ deep, 50″ high, 7″ back rail, late 1920s.

Chifforobe with two-tone striped mahogany veneer and painted facings, 36″ wide, 18″ deep, 54″ high, 1920s.

Chifforobe with striped walnut veneer top and sides, two-piece matched burl walnut veneer on doors and selected hardwood frame, 40″ wide, 20″ deep, 56″ high, 1920s.

Chifforette with burl mahogany veneer on doors and lower drawer and burl walnut veneer on upper drawers; there are three pull-out drawers behind the doors, 34″ wide, 19″ deep, 50″ high, 1920s.

Dresser made of selected hardwoods finished in a two-tone walnut with router lines and lightwood decorative panels on drawers, 45″ wide, 20″ deep, 67″ high, 1920s.

Chiffonier with bird's-eye maple veneer and selected hardwoods, 31" wide, 21" deep, 74" high, 1920s.

From early times wooden box-type chests were present in homes, but in the 1920s a different type prevailed. Cedar chests with their fragrant scent appeared and the first versions generally seemed to be those with cedar all the way - outside as well as within. Frequently, they had wide copper bands on the outside. Some were of walnut veneer or stained gumwood with a Tennessee cedar lining. Many of the chests have their labels intact inside the lid and one company emphasized that it used no imitation

Child's cedar chest, 30" wide, 14" deep, 13" high; regular size cedar chest, 40" wide, 19" deep, 18" high, made by Caswell-Runyan, Cabinet Makers, 1920s.

veneers or woods. As the 1920s terminated, cedar chests generally stood on small turned legs and had plain inscribed lines. Sometimes imitation four-way matched burl walnut overlays were found on genuine walnut veneer tops or fronts.

Owners should check locks and hinges for patent dates or numbers. A Lane cedar chest pictured in the book has the patent number 1,759,401 on its lock. This figure indicates that the lock was patented in 1930. The Lane Company, Inc., Altavista, Virginia, makers of a complete line of cedar chests, stated they adhered to government recommendations for moth killing cedar chests. Seventy percent of each chest, including the back, front, ends and bottom was built of aromatic red cedar heartwood three-fourths of an inch thick.

In the early 1930s, cedar chests had turned legs. Overlay veneers appeared in curly or bird's-eye maple and satinwood. Sometimes expensive burl rosewood overlays were used. Carved moldings or zebrawood borders with fibrewood carvings were not uncommon. When a rail appeared at the back, the result was called a window seat cedar chest. In 1933, cedar chests were offered in several styles by the Rockford Eagle Furniture Company, Rockford, Illinois. It was possible to secure from this firm console types or window seats in Queen Anne, Spanish, Italian Renaissance and Jacobean period designs. Around the middle of the 1930s, versions with waterfall fronts came into prominence. Most cedar chests had turned legs but a tendency toward squaring off at the base was apparent. By the late thirties the majority avoided legs per se, replacing them with an apron-type base. Catalogue descriptions of cedar chest veneer patterns included sliced walnut tops and ends, Orientalwood fronts with claro crotched veneer center panels bordered with zebrawood. Also named were four-way matched claro tops and fronts with striped walnut ends and Oriental panels.

In the early 1940s, some cedar chests had pin striped waterfall tops. Veneers displayed on the fronts were matched paldao, claro and figured or four-way matched butt walnut. As the 1940s came to a close, cedar chests with unusual veneers and waterfall fronts were still present, although a trend toward a squaring off of the tops began. Sliced prima vera with diamond matched prima vera and diamond-matched zebrawood center bordered with marquetry inlay and spindled carved molding described one chest. Some types had lift-out hinged trays. A buyer might prefer a waterfall top and ends of sliced walnut veneer or V-matched tops of striped and crotch walnut with diamond-matched tigerwood overlay, spindled carved trim and genuine marquetry inlay. One company advertised a mahogany veneered chest with Chippendale legs and hardware and a shallow carved apron.

Cedar chest with plain-cut walnut veneer, poplar oval overlay in center with genuine Tennessee cedar interior lining, 48″ wide, 19″ deep, 21″ high, 1920s, made by Forest Park Chests, Forest Park, Illinois.

Window-seat cedar chest with plain-cut walnut veneer top and sides, figured walnut veneer front and applied decorations, 48″ wide, 19″ deep, 21″ high, 1930s, made by Lane Company, Inc., Alta Vista, Virginia.

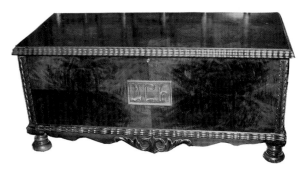

Cedar chest with a label stating that the cabinet was made with American and Oriental walnut veneers, 45″ wide, 19″ deep, 20″ high, late 1920s.

Waterfall cedar chest with label stating, "All veneers used on the exterior are of the finest genuine American and Oriental wood," which says that the veneers are from the walnut family because Orientalwood is, in reality, a type of walnut from Australia, 46″ wide, 18″ deep, 23″ high, late 1930s, made by the Billington Manufacturing Company, Sheboygan, Wisconsin.

Cedar chest with V-matched Macassar ebony veneer on front and applied decorations, 48″ wide, 19″ deep, 21″ high, 1930s.

Waterfall cedar chest with satinwood, American and Oriental walnut veneers, 46″ wide, 19″ deep, 22″ high, middle 1930s.

Blanket chest with straight-cut mahogany veneer on top, two-tone bird's-eye maple veneer on front and selected hardwood case, 40″ wide, 18″ deep, 20″ high, 1930s.

Cedar chest covered with mohair upholstery, 36″ wide, 20″ deep, 19″ high, late 1930s.

Waterfall cedar chest with satinwood veneer top and center panel, zebrawood veneer banding and mottled lacewood front side panels, 44″ wide, 18″ deep, 22″ high, 1938.

The following excerpt from the 1927 Sears, Roebuck catalogue calls attention to the importance of cedar chests by comparing them to low cost insurance protection.

"Compare the costs of one of these beautiful cedar chests with the cost of one winter overcoat or a fur coat or a pair of woolen blankets! No other insurance gives protection against actual loss! No other insurance requires one cash payment and you are covered for the rest of your life! We believe that no matter where you look, you won't find more beautiful, more dependable, more practical chests than these for anything like our low prices. Insure your woolen and furs with the premium of a cedar chest."

Following is a list of some companies that made cedar chests:

Billing Manufacturing Company, Sheboygan, Wisconsin
Coswell-Runyan Company, Huntington, Indiana
Dillingham Lakeside, Sheboygan, Wisconsin
Eagle Furniture Company, Rockford, Illinois
Forest Park Chests, Forest Park, Illinois
Franklin Shockey, Lexington, South Carolina
Klein Brothers, Long Island City, New York
Landau Cabinet Company, St. Louis, Missouri
The Lane Company, Inc., Altavista, Virginia
Seaburg Manufacturing Company, Jamestown, New York
Stewart Company, Norwalk, Ohio
Tennessee Furniture Corporation, Chattanooga, Tennessee
Tennessee Red Cedar & Novelty Company, Chattanooga, Tennessee
West Branch Novelty Company, Milton, Oregon

The new types of furniture introduced in the 1920s were more diminutive than those found in homes of the late 1800s. Carving glamorized 19th century solid woods, but the exotic veneers of the decades surrounding and including the depression years provided their own decorative effects.

Bathrooms changed bedroom furniture requirements. No longer were washstands and commodes required. New types of furniture including the chifforobe and chifforette received emphasis. Vanities added dramatic touches and cedar chests were valuable storage units. The bed chamber name changed. It became a bedroom.

Poster bed with Oriental walnut and satinwood veneers on headboard and footboard, applied decorations and a selected hardwood frame, 62″ high at headpost; 55″ high at footpost, 1930s. Part of a four-piece set including chest of drawers, vanity and bench (not pictured).

Chest of drawers with two-tone V-matched paldao veneer on two bottom drawers, satinwood veneer on top drawers of bottom section and top drawer of upper section and two-tone V-matched Orientalwood veneer on bottom drawer in upper section and applied decorations; bottom drawer is cedar-lined, 36″ wide, 18″ deep, 68″ high, 1930s. Part of a four-piece set including poster bed, vanity and bench (not pictured).

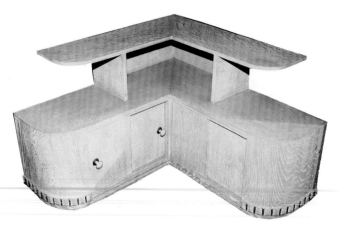

Corner bookshelf and cabinet with limed oak finish and four sliding doors, 34″ wide from front to corner, 11″ deep, 23″ high, 1940s. Part of a four-piece set including vanity (not pictured), bench and chifforobe.

Vanity with two-tone Orientalwood veneer on outside drawers and beneath mirror, satinwood veneer on three smaller drawers and applied decoration, 48″ wide, 18″ deep, 69″ high, 1930s. Part of a four-piece set including poster bed, chest of drawers and bench (not pictured).

Vanity bench with limed oak finish, 20″ wide, 14″ deep, 22″ high, 1940s. Part of a four-piece set including vanity (not pictured), corner bookshelf and cabinet and chifforobe.

Vanity bench with striped walnut veneer and selected hardwoods, 24″ wide, 14″ deep, 18″ high, late 1940s.

Chifforobe with limed oak finish and celluloid knobs, 33″ wide, 18″ deep, 47″ high on drawer side, 53″ high by doors, 1940s. Part of a four-piece set including vanity (not pictured), corner bookshelf and cabinet and vanity bench.

Vanity chair with diamond-matched satinwood veneer back and selected hardwood frame, 25″ arm to arm, 32″ high, 1938, made by the W.M. Bassett Furniture Company, Martinsville, Virginia.

Vanity chair with V-matched quarter-sliced Zebrawood veneer and striped zebrawood veneer on back, 28″ arm to arm, 31″ high, late 1930s.

Vanity bench with walnut veneer and selected hardwoods, 27″ wide, 16″ deep, 18″ high, 1930. Part of a two-piece set including dressing table with large round mirror (not pictured).

Vanity chair with V-matched African walnut veneer on back and apron and selected hardwood frame, 30″ high, early 1940s.

Bed with paldao veneer panels, router lines and hand-painted floral design, 56″ wide, 45″ high headboard, 29″ high footboard, early 1930s.

97

Commode washstand with bird's-eye maple veneer and selected hardwoods, 1920s.

Chest of drawers with V-matched Orientalwood and satinwood veneer on two top drawers, basketweave zebrawood and burl walnut veneer on bottom three drawers and selected hardwood frame, 36″ wide, 20″ deep, 53″ high, 1930s. Part of a three-piece set including bed and dresser that are not pictured.

Chest-on-chest with matched and V-matched Oriental walnut and bird's-eye maple veneer on drawer fronts, router lines, applied decorations and hand-painted floral deisgn on overlay oval panel, 36″ wide, 19″ deep, 52″ high, early 1930s. Part of a four-piece set including bed, vanity and vanity stool that are not pictured.

Waterfall chest of drawers with V-matched and diamond-matched plain sliced red gum veneer on drawer fronts, maple overlay panel on top drawer and horizontal bandings of zebrawood veneer, 1930s, made by Graham Brothers, Inc., Chicago. Part of a three-piece set including bed and dresser, pictured in this chapter, made by another furniture manufacturer.

Twin bed with four-piece matching burl walnut veneer, applied decorations and selected hardwood frame, 42″ wide, 50″ high headboard, 30″ high footboard, 1930s, made by the Table Rock Furniture Company, Morgantown, North Carolina. There is another matching twin bed.

Night stand with plain-sliced figured maple veneer and selected hardwoods, 17″ wide, 14″ deep, 30″ high, 1920s.

Bed with figured walnut veneer, bird's-eye maple overlays, router lines and selected hardwood frame, 57″ wide, 52″ high headboard, 1930s.

Night stand painted ivory and blue with applied decorations, 17″ wide, 14″ deep, 28″ high, 1920s, made by the Sligh Furniture Company, Grand Rapids, Michigan.

Commode with plain striped mahogany veneer top and banding beneath top and V-matched veneer drawer fronts, 15″ wide, 14″ deep, 27″ high, 1930s.

Night stand made of solid cherry, 22″ wide, 15″ deep, 28″ high, 1930s, made by Willet.

Console with plain-cut mahogany veneer top, crotch mahogany veneer door, drawer and panels, 26″ wide, 13″ deep, 31″ high, 1930s, made by Imperial Furniture Company, Grand Rapids, Michigan.

Vanity desk with plain-cut walnut veneer top, sides, drawer front and selected hardwood base, 34″ wide, 21″ deep, 70″ high, 1920s.

Chapter Seven

The Student's Corner

Magazine baskets (or holders) and racks, bookcases, desks - these are articles of furniture found in the student's corner. Magazine baskets were diminutive, squat holders that sat on the floor near a comfortable chair or sofa where their contents were within easy reach of the reader. The racks were erect stationary bookcases. Although there was a distinction between the two, both were referred to as stands.

The little baskets frequently featured handles so they could be toted when necessary. Early ones often had a decorated, colored panel on the front - a boat, flowers, a windmill or some enticing print. Red and green lacquered examples with appropriate figures of people, gardens or buildings produced an Oriental flair. Prices in the early 1930s for common varieties ranged from ninety five cents to two dollars and twenty nine cents. The more expensive kinds frequently had additional pockets (divisions to separate magazines). If you wanted to save money or had the creative urge, you could invest sixty-five cents and decorate your own.

Mail-order houses warned prospective purchasers to include postage on mailable items that were sent flat and were advertised as "easily set up"; hence, amateur carpenter skills were required before these products could be used. If wood lacked appeal, metal magazine holders, available with either solid or lacy sides were sold. By the 1940s, painting waned style-wise and plain veneered walnut or mahogany stands prevailed. Some were made of gum or other hardwoods stained walnut.

Two-pocket magazine basket (holder or stand) with hand-painted Dutch motif, 14" wide, 10" deep, 26" high, late 1920s.

End table with magazine basket, 23" wide, 11" deep, 23" high, 1920s.

One-pocket magazine basket, 16″ wide, 7″ deep, 23″ high, 1920s.

Two-pocket magazine basket, 16″ wide, 8″ deep, 21″ high, 1920s.

Two-pocket magazine basket with hand-painted parrot motif on front, 15″ wide, 7″ deep, 22″ high, 1920s.

Two-pocket magazine basket with mahogany veneer, 18″ wide, 11″ deep, 18″ high, 1920s, made by Ferguson Brothers Manufacturing Company, Hoboken, New Jersey.

Two-pocket metal magazine basket, 11″ wide, 8″ deep, 19″ high, 1920s.

Two-pocket magazine basket with gum veneer finished walnut, 14″ wide, 18″ deep, 21″ high, 1940s.

Students, of course, require places to put books and a stack type case was produced that allowed for growth since six separate units could be purchased individually. For example, enclosed shelves had glass door fronts that pushed up and back to open or pulled out and down to close. A top piece and a footed base completed the stack. Sometimes a drawer was incorporated in the base. One large manufacturer of sectional bookcases was Globe-Wernicke of Cincinnati. This firm produced many in oak, but later offered mahogany veneered types.

Bookcase of mahogany and mahogany veneer, 52" wide, 16" deep, 56" high, 1920s, made by the Grand Rapids Chair Company, Grand Rapids, Michigan.

Stack bookcase of mahogany and mahogany veneer, 51" wide, 11" deep, 62" high, 1920s, made by Globe-Wernicke, Cincinnati, Ohio.

Gunn, another producer of sectional bookcases, originated in Grand Rapids, Michigan, as the Gunn Folding Bed Company in 1890 and became Gunn Furniture Company eight years later. One of their oak sectional bookcases was recently seen with Dec. 5, 1899 and Jan. 1, 1901 as the two listed patent dates. The firm name appeared frequently in the 1930s on birch or golden oak bookcases and on golden oak rolltop desks with writing surfaces varying in width from 48" to 60".

The bookcases with heavy scrolled feet and pilasters, made in the 1920s, were copies of 1840 Late Empire pieces that the furniture manufacturers of the 1920s called Colonial. Oddly enough, since companies called their products whatever they chose, a very different type of furniture made of darkened maple or sometimes birch, with simple lines and no scrolls was designated Colonial in the late 1930s. The name was evidently for sales appeal, not because it had any close resemblance to pre-1776 hand-crafted furniture fashioned during the days when the colonies, not the United States, existed.

Double type cases with two doors were commodious. When they had adjustable shelves, they accommodated books of various heights easily. Glass door panes were enhanced with wooden fretwork patterns. At times it is difficult to distinguish a bookcase from a china cabinet. The latter usually had an incised line running lengthwise near the back edge of the shelves to permit pretty plates to be positioned in a precise row. This clue helps because books don't require a router line for support.

Desks came in many styles - drop lids, table top, spinet, traditional period copies, secretaries, kneeholes or Art Moderne. Some had further generic titles such as Governor Winthrop, blockfront, breakfront or waterfall.

The desk evolved from a portable box that held writing materials. It had a slant top that served as a writing surface. At first the hinges were at the rear and since the top lifted up away from the user, its always had to be cleared before the lid was raised. Gradually, hinges added to the front, resulted in drop lid versions that were much more convenient since the clutter was concealed within. The inclusion of a frame with legs and later drawers at the base increased the functions of the piece. Eventually, on some versions, bookcases incorporated on top provided even more space and these tall desks were called secretaries.

A creative way to form a desk was to convert an existing piece of furniture. That's what happened to an early stringed musical instrument called a spinet, a Colonial Period ancestor of the piano. When the instrument wore out, the keyboard was sometimes removed and the cabinet was transformed into a desk. Manufacturers around the early 1930s copied this idea to create their own versions of the spinet desk. Since it was not a ponderous piece, it could be used in almost any area.

Spinet desk of solid mahogany, 39″ wide, 21″ deep, 33″ high, 1920s, made by the Colonial Manufacturing Company.

Historically, there were several Governor Winthrops in the English colonies. For some reason that name has become attached to typical drop-lid desks of the Chippendale period even though all the governors (grandfather, father, son) pre-date that style by well over half a century. Have you read about the Puritan John Winthrop who headed the Massachusetts Bay Colony after his arrival from England in 1630? His namesake son and grandson

Governor Winthrop desk of mahogany veneer and solid mahogany with fall front, serpetine front and two document compartments, 36″ wide, 19″ deep, 42″ high, 1920s.

both served as governors of Connecticut. Because the latter, John III, died in 1707, and the English cabinetmaker Chippendale was not born until 1717, these governmental leaders did not write on such desks. In addition, Chippendale's influence was not felt on this side of the Atlantic until about 1755 to 1790. This serves as evidence that names were conjured up at the whim of the manufacturer.

In 1929, three dozen furniture firms were located at Rockford, Illinois. Among these was the Skandia Furniture Company whose products included plain green lacquered secretaries or ones with red crackle decorated finishes. A secretary with a painted finish is illustrated.

Pediments were present on many Governor Winthrop secretaries. These were usually curved shapes such as scrolls or arches at the top of the bookcase. When the arch was disrupted in the middle, just short of the apex, a gap was provided for an ornamental finial. Since the arch was not continuous, it was called a broken pediment. If the front of the desk base wiggled like a snake in motion, it was classified as a serpentine front.

Governor Winthrop fall-front secretary of mahogany veneer and selected hardwoods with broken pediment, 33″ wide, 19″ deep, 79″ high, late 1920s.

Fall-front secretary with tiger maple veneer on pediment, drawer fronts and drop front with hardwood maple frame, 30" wide, 15" deep, 76" high, late 1930s, made by Frank and Son, Inc., Manufacturers of Furniture and House Furnishings, New York.

Fall-front secretary with tiger maple veneer on pediment, serpentine drawer fronts and fall front with hardwood maple frame, 32" wide, 16" deep, 80" high, late 1920s, made by Maddox Tables, Germantown, New York.

Fall-front secretary with broken pediment and block front drawers, 30" wide, 15" deep, 78" high, 1927.

Blockfronts are considered an American contribution to desks, chests, cabinets or other case pieces. They originated in the 1760s-1780s and are associated with the work of John Goddard, his son-in-law John Townsend and other craftsmen of the Newport, Rhode Island area. They were also made in Massachusetts and Connecticut. The fronts of these pieces were broken vertically into three distinct raised panels or blocks from which the name is derived. This style-setter was emulated by manufacturers of the late 1920s.

When a desk is finished on the back as well as on the front, it does not have to assume a wallflower position in a room. Instead of being backed against a wall, it can extend into the room.

A knee-hole desk allows space for a sitter to place his legs between two rows of drawers or doors on either side of a flat topped writing surface. There are sometimes versions with storage space on only one side or with a narrow cupboard at the back of the feet section. The important emphasis is to allow room for the knees.

Knee-hole desk with green leather-tooled top, sliced mahogany veneer sides and back and burl mahogany veneer drawer fronts, 48" wide, 26" deep, 30" high, early 1940s.

Bleached woods became popular around the 1940s. Walnut or mahogany was lightened in color or sometimes an actual wood with a light tone such as holly, sycamore or satinwood was used. A paper label inside the drawer of a bleached mahogany veneer and birch base desk, pictured here, states, "This furniture is finished with a special material capable of withstanding repeated washings and accidental spillings of alcohol, iodine, ink and other ordinary chemicals. It will not chip or craze. Exercising reasonable care this furniture will give life time satisfaction." It was signed by The Hill-Rom Company, Batesville, Indiana. With just that information it can be surmised that the desk was manufactured after 1933 since the reference to alcohol stain suggests that it was produced after prohibition was revoked. If you are old enough to remember the sting of iodine applied to childhood cuts and scrapes (ouch!), you know the desk is an old timer. Although, the piece is not as yet a bona fide 100-year-old antique, it's half way there.

Music rack designed and finished to resemble bamboo with examples of vintage clothes and jewelry, 17" wide, 12" deep, 37" high, 1920s.

Knee-hole desk with plain-sliced walnut veneer top, sides and panels and figured walnut veneer drawer fronts and stiles and solid walnut legs, 42" wide, 33" deep, 30" high, early 1930s.

Table desk with bleached mahogany top, sides and drawer front and birch hardwood base, 36" wide, 18" deep, 30" high, early 1940s.

Desk with figured mahogany veneer framing leather inset on top, figured mahogany veneer on drawer fronts, sides and back and selected hardwood legs, 43" wide, 23" deep, 29" high, 1930s.

Desk with checker-board marquetry top, 34" wide, 22" deep, 30" high, 1938, made at the Lake Geneva, Wisconsin, Franciscan Monastery and signed "Brother (B.R.) B.A."

Desk chair with painted and decorated Chinese theme, 38" high, early 1930s. Part of a two-piece set including desk.

Waterfall front knee-hole desk with Oriental veneer top, sides and artificially grained drawer fronts with veneerite decorations, late 1930s.

Desk with painted and decorated Chinese theme, 38" wide, 22" deep, 42" high, early 1930s. Part of a two-piece set including chair.

Sheraton-type desk with sliced mahogany veneer top and sides, curly maple veneer apron and drawer fronts with selected hardwood legs, 1930s, marked Colby's D 5431.

Desk with satinwood veneer top, Macassar ebony and bird's-eye maple veneer small drawer fronts, stumpwood walnut veneer on large drawer fronts and Macassar ebony veneer beneath drawers, 50" wide, 19" deep, 30" high, late 1930s.

Drop-lid desk with mahogany veneer top, sides, drop lid, drawer front and apron and selected hardwood base, 30″ wide, 16″ deep, 68″ high, 1920s.

Drop-lid desk with plain-sliced walnut veneer top and sides and figured walnut veneer drop lid and drawer fronts and selected hardwood frame, 31″ wide, 16″ deep, 63″ high, 1920s.

Table top desk with bird's-eye maple veneer top and drawer front and maple base, 36″ wide, 19″ deep, 31″ high, 1920s, made by Innes Pearce & Company, Rushville, Indiana.

Chest desk with plain-sliced walnut veneer top and sides and butt walnut veneer door fronts with maple and mahogany overlays, 31″ wide, 15″ deep, 42″ high, 1920s, made by the Skandia Furniture Company, Rockford, Illinois.

Chapter Eight

Miscellaneous Furnishings and Accessories

Buffet, mantle or landscape, console, gesso, artificial grain, Venetian, etched, engraved, polychrome, bevel, filigree, convex - these terms have a common denominator. They are all associated with mirrors, much used accessories of the 1920s, 1930s and 1940s. The three terms buffet, mantle and landscape were the picturesque manner in which various companies described mirrors with a series of panels, normally three or four, that were wide rather than high. They will be called buffet mirrors in the text in spite of the fact that they were not assigned to any one area in the home but were appropriate for the hall, living room or dining area. Their frames were ornate but narrow, and the glass itself was usually etched at the top edge with tiny flowers or garlands. Venetian glasses also wore hazy looking etched decorations created by the corrosive action of hydrofluoric acid. There were long buffet types or tall consoles. Usually they were not framed, but some had a partial frame in the form of a decorative top. Engraved cut lines, sharper than the shadowy-appearing etched designs, were frequently present.

Popular, pretty polychrome work, meaning decorated with many colors, added soft-hued touches to frames, to metal lamp bases and smoker stands or to applied furniture decorations. Pottery and porcelain had polychrome applications, too.

Console is a word that has gone through transformations. Originally, it referred to a wall bracket that was a support for cornices or shelves. Later, it included tables attached to the wall with leg supports at the front only. Because graceful, tall mirrors were the common companions over these tables, they accepted the title console mirrors. Many mirrors have a slant, called a bevel, at the edge where they fit into the frame. Such a bevel can appear on wood, metal or other materials as well.

Filigree formerly denoted dainty decorations in wire, especially of gold or silver. It came to be applied generally to any delicate, light, lace-like ornamental work of that nature. Gesso has a more humble association because it has a plaster-of-Paris base formed into slightly raised (bas relief) designs. It is sometimes molded, carved, sculptured, painted or gilted. Frames were frequently candidates for such treatment and some frames were artificially grained to imitate a certain wood. Photographs in this chapter demonstrate some of these characteristics.

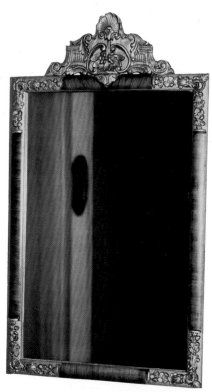

Polychrome console mirror with burnished gold and artificially grained frame, 14" wide, 24" high, 1930s.

Buffet mirror with beveled glass, etched designs and burnished gold frame, 46″ wide, 16″ high, late 1920s.

Console mirror with beveled glass and burnished gold frame, 16″ wide, 30″ high, 1930s.

Polychrome frame with burnished gold and artificial graining showing a camel scene by Buxton, 23″ wide, 18″ high, 1934.

Console mirror with beveled glass, etched designs and leaf and scroll crest, 13″ wide, 28″ high, 1920s.

Polychrome frame with artificial graining, 13″ wide, 19″ high, 1930s.

Tapestry with burnished and artificially grained frame depicting Colonial Courtship. 60" wide, 26" high. Scenes on other tapestries include: Blind Man's Bluff, Farm Festival, Garden Scene, Tavern Scene, Dinner for Four, Flower Girl, Art Gallery and Inn Scene. 1920s.

Impressed by the power of the radio, a 1936 encyclopedia states there were 625 licensed broadcasting stations in the nation in that year and proudly boasted that if an event of unusual importance occurred, as many as 200 stations could be linked together in a single hook-up! Chains of 20 to 30 stations were not uncommon. A brief history of broadcasting is given in Chapter Two.

Many people purchased kits and made their own crystal sets during the 1920s and 1930s, but companies sold completed radios as well. A brass label with a patent date of 1926-1927 appears on the top of a metal Atwater Kent radio. An avid collector stated that it is unusual to locate one that has its original metal stand intact. The one illustrated is a complete unit with the speaker sitting on the bottom shelf of the stand.

Oftentimes, radios have patent numbers on them. By examining a chart included in this book that lists patent numbers and their corresponding dates, the patent year can be ascertained. By this means it was determined that a Crosley radio pictured in this chapter was patented in 1931. According to a paper label on its wooden cabinet, Showers Brothers were "Makers of furniture for the homes of America since 1868. Signed by W. Edw Showers". Another statement reads, "The design of this console has been approved. The manufacturer has been selected and is authorized to sell it through Crosley jobbers and dealers. Powel Crosley, Jr." That's impressive to have both the radio manufacturer and the cabinet maker's signatures still intact. Showers Brothers Company, Bloomington, Indiana, offered radio furniture in blistered maple, zebrawood, Oriental walnut, satinwood and many other veneers.

Atwater Kent radio and speaker with original metal polychrome stand, 17" wide, 11" deep, 35" high, patented 1926-1927.

Crosley radio with plain-sliced walnut veneer on top and sides and four-piece matching burl walnut veneer on doors with selected hardwood frame, 25" wide, 18" deep, 43" high, 1931; cabinet was made by Showers Brothers Company, Bloomfield, Indiana, Bloomington, Indiana and Burlington, Iowa.

An article by Earl Reeves in the May 20, 1926 issue of *The Youth's Companion* magazine is entitled "The Boys Who Made Radio". It relates the following facts. When Powel Crosley, Jr.'s son and namesake wanted a radio in 1921, his dad felt $130 was too much to pay. Instead, he read an instruction book, and he and his son built a crystal set for $35. The father became convinced sets could be made for people with lean billfolds by making large quantities and selling them cheaper. "Harko Junior", a crystal set, was followed by "Harko Senior", a one tube set. The article continued, "Today (in 1926) he (Crosley) makes every single part that goes into his sets in his own factory" with its 1,200 employees.

When radios no longer function, housewives who find their cabinets too attractive to discard, preserve them. The radio parts are removed and shelves are inserted to form a utilitarian storage unit. An example is pictured.

Art Moderne Westinghouse clock radio with two-tone plain-sliced walnut veneer front panel, 15" wide, 12" deep, 62" high, middle 1930s.

On the top of the step table radio is a Frankart bronzed metal ash tray with a bird incorporated in the design. Frankart, Inc. of New York, New York, created metal lamps, bookends and ash trays in the 1920s, often with a green cast to simulate verdigris, a natural green patina on copper, brass or bronze.

Radio cabinet with four-piece matching stumpwood walnut veneer on door, applied decorations and selected hardwood frame, 26" wide, 18" deep, 55" high, early 1930s.

Some unusual radio forms were produced and are pictured here. One resembles a tall case clock with a time piece at the top and a Westinghouse radio at the base. Another with an Art Moderne feel is a radio in a mahogany step table case sold by Philco.

Philco end table radio with plain-sliced walnut veneer case, 15" wide, 24" deep, 22" high, late 1930s. Two accessories include Frankart ashtray and brass magazine holder.

The Litl Boy Crosley radio with plain-sliced walnut veneer top and sides, figured walnut and maple veneers on front and selected hardwood frame, 21″ wide, 12″ deep, 35″ high, middle 1930s.

Coronado floor model radio with figured walnut veneer case and selected hardwood decorations, 21″ wide, 11″ deep, 36″ high, late 1930s. Chromium framed clock on onyx base, 10″ wide, 4″ deep, 10″ high, made by Manning-Bowman.

Sentinel sofa radio with plain-sliced walnut veneer and selected hardwood case, 21″ wide, 13″ deep, 21″ high, late 1930s. A radio of this type was placed by the arm of a sofa.

Majestic radio with plain-sliced walnut veneer top and sides, butt walnut veneer front and stiles and selected hardwood frame, 25″ wide, 16″ deep, 38″ high, middle 1930s, made by Grigsby-Grunow. The clock is a Plymouth eight-day, 13″ wide, 4″ deep, 9″ high, 1940s, made in Thomaston, Connecticut.

A dial twister liked to have a place to sit while tuning in to a favorite program. Small, pull-up radio benches that some people called fireside benches performed this function. They varied in designs and in the materials used. A wooden base was simple and upholstered tops were common. Fancier benches had cast steel bases with old bronze finishes, polychrome touches or legs enhanced by lyre designs or curves. Two examples are illustrated.

Radio or fireside bench with polychrome metal frame, 24″ wide, 11″ deep, 24″ high, 1930s.

Radiobench with copperwashed metal frame, 23″ wide, 12″ deep, 16″ high, 1930s.

Chapter Nine

Accent on Oak

Approximately 275 known varieties of oak spread their branches in countries all around the world. Of these, sixty types are native to the United States, but only about fourteen are important as furniture woods and are primarily from the regions east of the Great Plains. Oak of some type, from shrubs to trees, grows in almost every wooded area in the nation, but those used extensively in the construction of furniture are white and red oak.

The grain patterns of oak differ according to the way the lumber is cut. Quarter sawing results in a vivid pattern because oak's large medullary rays are exposed. Referred to as flakes, they are the largest in any tree indigenous to the United States. When a log is plain sawed, the figure appears as straight lines or ellipitical V's. It is not so pronounced a pattern as that produced by quarter sawing but both these cuts of oak lumber are desirable in furniture making.

Extension table with quarter-sawed oak top, apron and solid oak legs and stationary center leg support, 54″ wide, 45″ deep, 30″ high, 1920s.

Woods are classified as either hard or soft. Trees with needles are called soft woods and because they bear cones, they are called coniferous trees. In contrast, hardwoods are deciduous trees, a type that sheds its broad leaves. Some are open grained, including oak. Others are closed grained. Novices in wood identification rarely realize that what seems to be oak may not be. There are other species with a similar appearance.

The species of trees that share some of oak's characteristics are ash, chestnut, elm and hickory. A fifth look-alike emerges when an inexpensive, light toned wood is given an artificial oak grain. Furniture with this type of graining was available for those who could not afford the genuine product but who desired to follow the fashion trends of the times. The hotel trade provided another outlet for this substitute oak grain.

The imitation results when color is stroked on a piece of furniture with special brushes, rollers, combs or other graining devices. If refinishing is attempted on furniture with a sham finish, paint remover will obliterate the false grain. That chameleon-like switch can be a shock to someone who thought the piece was pure oak. On furniture made of solid wood (not veneered), inspect both the inside and outside of the panels and underneath the top to see whether the same type of wood prevails throughout. If the grain pattern on the outside resembles oak but the inside pattern differs, it is possible to suspect false graining. Worn off places around drawer handles may provide a clue that the grain pattern was artificially applied.

The quartet of trees that share oak's characteristics can be people foolers. Many so-called oak ice boxes were actually made from ash or elm and are designated in this way in catalogues of the 1920s. In the 1920s and 1930s these two woods frequently were used in the construction of breakfast nook tables and chairs or of dinette sets. Both ash and elm blend well to form hoops or bows on chair backs. Carpathian and burl elm with their pleasing patterns are used as decorative veneers.

Chestnut trees, almost obliterated by a blight in the early 1900s, make attractive paneling, woodwork and picture frames.

Tough, supple hickory is important where strength is essential. It has an oak color and texture. Because of their different attributes, a piece of furniture may incorporate two or more of these stand-ins for oak, each one functioning where it can serve the best.

Walnut, oak, maple, birch, cherry, gumwood and pine are the leading American furniture woods. Because popularity is fickle, walnut and oak have switched leadership positions in past periods while the other species lagged behind.

A specific wood or style refuses to be confined within certain years. Instead, overlapping occurs. For example, oak, glowing golden, dark fumed or stained was king from 1890 to 1925. When the extensive use of veneers entered the industry near the end of the 1920s, native walnut and imported mahogany returned as veneers. They were joined by many other veneers with fancy names such as avodire, kelobra, lacewood, Orientalwood, sycamore and zebrawood. Seemingly the age of oak was past, but the king refused to accept this fact and did not abdicate. Retail stores still had some in stock and customers continued to seek it. Manufacturers had it available. The old style oak remained around through the 1920s, 1930s and to a limited extent, in the 1940s even though it was no longer the leading style.

Oak breakfast and dinette sets are illustrated in Chapter Four. It was an organizational puzzle for the authors to decide where these tables and chairs, introduced in the 1920s and 1930s, should be placed. Should they go in the kitchen-dining room chapter or, since they are made of oak or its look-alikes, should they go in this chapter? It was decided to place them in the former location.

Consider how handy it is to have extension tables. An old way to provide for extra guests was to move unmatched tables together to create one long one. Problems resulted when not all of them were the same height or width. Extension tables, available in various forms, avoided this hassle. Some have a middle leg that retains its position when the other legs pull outward to leave a space in the top for placing additional leaves. Frequently, pedestals separate to support the weight of an extended surface. Folded leaves may pop up from storage underneath the table top. Other extension tables have drop leaves while some table tops are double and the ends pull out and up to create a larger area. Shapes vary according to the type selected. Take your choice - round, square, oval or rectangular. The extension table is indeed functional.

Extension table with plain-sliced oak veneer top and quarter-sawed oak veneer apron and base, 42″ diameter, 28″ high, 1920s.

It is ironic that manufacturers of the 1920s advertised oak furniture they called Colonial. Such styles were produced by factories as the twentieth century commenced and, to some degree, retained their salable status through the depression era of the 1930s. The name colonial was a new advertising approach to help promote an old product. The term is not appropriate because this furniture does not resemble examples from the true Colonial period prior to 1776. Instead, the presence of pilasters and heavy scrolled feet apes the Empire designs of the late 1840s.

Any discussion of oak furniture should include the contributions of the Stickley family. Gustav Stickley (1857-1942) was influenced by the English Arts and Crafts Movement. He did away with carving, curves and extensive ornamentation and introduced stern, stocky, sturdy furniture instead. Straight slats, legs, and rungs were, to him, better than turned ones. He called his new stoic style Craftsman and presented it to the public in 1900 at the Grand Rapids Furniture Exposition. Gustav Stickley was disturbed when his generic name for it was not selected. After all, he was the innovator and he contended that his workmanship and designs were so well executed that they could not be improved. He consistently insisted that his products would increase many times over their original values in fifty to one hundred years. Lo - verily - his prophecy hath come true. Collectors pay well for his works. Unfortunately, although the Mission style overlapped into the depression era, Gustav Stickley's business did not. It went bankrupt in 1916.

Gustav Stickley resented the way other firms copied his styles. Most of all, he disliked the rivalry that developed when his younger brothers emulated his works, and their name appeared on furniture. It probably was a disappointment to Stickley when their firms continued to function after his failed.

Extension table of solid oak, 48" diameter, 29" high, with two leaves, 12" wide, 1920s, made by Quaint Furniture Stickley Brothers Company, Grand Rapids, Michigan.

His brother, Albert, was associated with Stickley Brothers Furniture Company, the home of Quaint Furniture. This organization advertised that it adapted English Arts and Crafts Movement ideas to develop furniture that offered its customers comfort, utility, simplicity and sincerity. The firm was established in 1883 and incorporated in 1891. In 1935, this manufacturing plant advertised truly modern furniture with the spirit of tomorrow, but according to the company, its design was based on a deep feeling for United States history. Pieces from this grouping were available in solid maple and in mahogany veneer.

Two other brothers in the furniture trade were known as L. & J.G. Stickley, Inc. Their main offices were located in Fayetteville, New York, and they produced high quality Mission styles. Customers who were too tall, too short, too stout or had other problems were offered customized furniture to meet their specific needs. Shortly after the company was founded in 1900, they manufactured furniture designed by Frank Lloyd Wright, the world renowned American architect. In the 1930s, this company, in touch with timely trends, made genuine Early American reproductions. Leopold and J. George advertised that the crafting of furniture was their only business. Collectors like to find any Stickley name on pieces even though Gustav Stickley's works are the ones that receive a standing ovation and command the high prices.

Library tables frequently held books, periodicals or newspapers. Lately, some have been cut down to serve as coffee tables, a fact that disturbs purists who prefer to leave furniture in it original state. Others feel that an owner should determine how an object best serves in a home's decor. Many of these library tables had heavy curved pillars and scrolled feet. The outline of a musical instrument, a lyre

without the strings, appeared on some. Often the tops were oval. Oak veneer tops were common, but artificial oak graining was frequently applied to less expensive versions.

Library table cut down to coffee table height with quarter-sawed top, apron, pillars and base and solid oak drawer, 42" wide, 26" deep, 22" high, 1920s.

Library table artificially grained to look like quarter-sawed oak, 48" wide, 28" deep, 29" high, 1920s.

Library table with quarter-sawed oak veneer top, pillars and base and solid oak apron and handleless drawer, 45" wide, 26" deep, 31" high, 1920s.

Library table of solid oak with lyre pillars and scroll feet, 40″ wide, 26″ deep, 30″ high, 1920s.

A library table had to have square lines to qualify for the Mission heading and those with shelves on the side were convenient for stacking books or magazines. A drawer, sometimes handleless, was generally included in the apron.

Mission library table with plain-sliced oak veneer top and selected hardwood base, 42″ wide, 26″ deep, 30″ high, 1920s.

Mission library table of solid oak, 43″ wide, 27″ deep, 30″ high, 1920s, made by Joerns Brothers Furniture, "Artistic Period Furniture", Stevens Point, Wisconsin.

Chairs, popular earlier in this century, with pressed designs of flowers, leaves, grotesques, fish or scrolls were passe in the 1920s. Generally, the turnings in the chair back, favored in the late 1800s and early 1900s, was replaced by one wide slat or a series of flat slats. In the mid-1930s or after, it was not unusual to find oak arm chairs with straight lines. A square panel in the back was upholstered to match the seat. Such styles, frequently with ribbing running up and down on the straight legs, continued through the 1940s. A very slight rounding sometimes appeared on the front of such legs.

Dining chair of solid oak, 38″ high, 1920s, made by Stomps-Burkhardt Company, "Modern Chairs of Quality", Dayton, Ohio.

Dining chair of solid oak, 40″ high, 1920s. One of a set of four.

118

Dining chair of solid oak, 37″ high, 1920s. One of a set of five.

China cabinet of quarter-sawed oak veneer, 48″ wide, 18″ deep, 64″ high, 1920s.

Dining chair of solid oak, 36″ high, middle 1930s. One of a set of six.

Oak china cabinets with convex glass sides, often with oak veneer covering a portion of their surface, were available. The straight type with the Empire scroll legs appeared, too. As the 1920s ended and the 1930s began, the cabinets had tall legs. Painted touches added flowers, baskets or other designs. One example pictured has etched fretwork on the doors and is merely marked "china" in black stenciled letters on the back. Hoosier cabinets were discussed in Chapter Four, but some that were not painted and are of oak are included here.

China cabinet of solid oak, 36″ wide, 12″ deep, 62″ high, 1920s.

China cabinet of quarter-sawed solid oak, 45" wide, 19" deep, 60" high, 1920s.

An intriguing name attached to a dainty bedroom storage piece is the phrase "princess dresser". Its base was not tall, but it had a generous sized swing mirror that allowed a female to see most of her figure. Do you suppose its petite and delicate appearing lines earned it the title, princess? A serpentine front dresser with two parallel drawers and a long drawer is illustrated.

A Square Brand dresser with quarter-sawed oak veneer was shown by Chittenden and Eastman Company of Burlington, Iowa. This firm has a history that dates back to 1866 when the business was established as H. Bailey & Company. Their motto read, "Furniture from everywhere, assembled in Burlington, ready to ship anywhere to-day." Currently, they retain their progressive image as wholesale distributors.

Dresser of quarter-sawed oak veneer, 40" wide, 21" deep, 70" high, 1920s, distributed by Chittenden & Eastman, "Square Brand Furniture", Burlington, Iowa. Part of a two-piece set including bed.

There were companies that referred to a bedroom dresser with a combination of drawers and doors, a mirror and a parallel towel bar as a hotel washstand. These are a definite carry-over from the past since urban areas had bathrooms and didn't need furniture of this nature. Small towns and rural areas

Princess dresser with quarter-sawed oak veneer top, plain-sliced oak veneer sides and drawer front and solid oak frame, 40" wide, 21" deep, 74" high, 1920s.

Hotel dresser of solid oak, 33" wide, 18" deep, 50" high, 1920s.

sometimes were without indoor plumbing until the 1940s; thus, the wash bowl, the pitcher and the emergency lidded pot required a place of their own. Many of these inexpensive washstands were artificially grained to resemble oak.

Hotel commode washstand of solid oak, 32″ wide, 18″ deep, 54″ high, 1920s.

In 1920, oak kitchen cabinets with glass enclosed doors at the top had line decorations. Their work surfaces were generally of metal or porcelain. Metal handles were present. Oak extension tables with a pedestal base either had square legs with a Mission feel or scroll legs similar to the 1840 Empire type. The massive claw, paw and lion-head feet belonged to the past.

In the bedrooms of the twenties, square dressers with legs frequently had either an imitation quarter-sawed finish or were fashioned of genuine quarter-sawed oak. Also available were oak vanities and semi-vanities.

Many chairs and rockers were of golden oak. When a sewing rocker had a drawer under the seat, it provided a place to keep material and thread. A massive golden oak rocker with rolled arms and a veneer rolled seat was comfortable, especially for a person with a bulky build. A flat, squared Mission look was seen on office chairs, swivel chairs, arm chairs and on golden oak rockers with leatherette upholstered seats.

Petite oak desks that were often called ladies' desks in previous years were listed in the 1920s under the heading of house desks.

A 1931 catalogue mentions ash tables and elm chairs as well as oak examples. Splayed legs were turned and dainty. One description of an oak dinette set said that butt walnut veneer panels decorated the doors of buffets and china cabinets. All solid parts were of genuine Appalachian oak. Pollard oak was an overlay used to enhance expensive sets. Many dining sets with refectory tables were fashioned from oak. The fronts of the buffets were carved generously and applied decorations were used. These solid wood relief carvings took the place of the elaborate veneers that enhanced walnut furniture of the mid-1930s. More expensive oak sets had Carpathian elm, quilted poplar or quarter-sawed American curly ash on drawer fronts.

Extension table with quarter-sawed oak veneer top, apron, pillar and base, 48″ diameter, 30″ high with two leaves, 9″ wide, 1920s.

Five-leg extension table of solid oak, 49″ wide, 44″ deep, 30″ high, 1920s.

Draw or refectory table with plain-sliced oak veneer top and solid oak base, 54″ wide, 36″ deep, 31″ high, 1930s.

Library table of solid oak, 38″ wide, 24″ deep, 31″ high, 1920s.

China cabinet made of solid oak with enameled designs, 36″ wide, 13″ deep, 69″ high, early 1930s, made by Levine Furniture Company, Cincinnati, Ohio.

Even in the 1940s some golden oak and Mission remained on the furniture scene. Frequently, solid oak kitchen chairs and Vienna bentwood types shone with a golden gloss. A limed oak finish was popular. In a 1949 catalogue, all exposed parts of a genuine oak bedroom set had a limed oak lacquer finish. With the exception of the vanity, all the case pieces, including the bed, would line up if placed together. The statement is also made that oak varies in color, some parts being darker than others. These variations do not indicate a defect, but are natural characteristics of oak wood. Perhaps it is because oak does have a vivid pattern and is available in different finishes that it attracts a following and earns its place, along with walnut, as one of the two leading native American furniture woods.

Hoosier-type kitchen cabinet of solid oak, 42″ wide, 26″ deep, 71″ high, 1920s.

Hoosier-type kitchen cabinet of solid oak with frosted glass panels, 40″ wide, 24″ deep, 69″ high, 1920s.

Dressing table with oak veneer top, drawer fronts and solid oak base, 32″ wide, 19″ deep, 60″ high, 1920s.

Sideboard or buffet of solid oak, 42″ wide, 20″ deep, 55″ high, 1920s.

Dresser of solid oak, 40″ wide, 20″ deep, 67″ high, 1920s.

Mission bed of solid oak, 56″ wide, 52″ high headboard, 40″ high footboard, 1920s.

Bedside stand with oak veneer top and solid oak drawer fronts and base, 25″ wide, 17″ deep, 32″ high, 1920s.

Chiffonier of solid oak with hat compartment, 33″ wide, 18″ deep, 67″ high, 1920s.

Chest of drawers with oak veneer sides, drawer fronts and solid oak top and frame, 31″ wide, 21″ deep, 39″ high, 1920s.

Chest of drawers of quarter-sawed oak veneer, 36″ wide, 18″ deep, 45″ high, 1920s.

Mission oak desk of solid oak, 29″ wide, 15″ deep, 41″ high, 1920s.

Drop-lid oak desk, 30″ wide, 15″ deep, 40″ high, 1920s.

Bookcase with oak veneer door fronts and solid oak frame, 43″ wide, 12″ deep, 57″ high, 1920s.

Mission oak umbrella stand of solid oak with drip pan missing, 12″ square, 28″ high, 1920s.

Three-pocket magazine basket of oak and oak veneer, 17″ wide, 8″ deep, 34″ high, 1920s.

126

Chapter Ten

Repairing and Replacing Veneer

Because the majority of the furniture manufactured during the 1920s, 1930s and 1940s was either partially or totally veneered, the restoration of a piece from this period may require the repairing or replacement of loose, damaged or missing veneer.

If possible you should know what kind of veneer was used on the piece you are repairing so you can achieve a match when ordering a replacement piece. However, because most veneers were colored by any of a multitude of stains or dyes, it will not always be possible to accurately identify the veneer by name. If this is the case, look at its present color and grain characteristics and match it with the veneers shown in Chapter 2 of this book. These samples were photographed in their natural state without the addition of any color or stain.

If you are a "do-it-yourselfer", you may wish to undertake the job; otherwise, send it to a professional restorer. This can entail a great expense because it is a time-consuming process, therefore, you must decide whether the piece needing repair justifies this cost.

Learning to repair veneer is not an impossible task if you carefully follow the procedures that are outlined.

Materials and Tools Needed

1. single edge razor blade
2. metal straight edge
3. white or hide glue
4. wax paper
5. various sizes of gluing blocks
6. clamps (C, spring and bar)
7. oil colors
8. varnish or other finish
9. clean cloths or paper towels
10. container of water
11. artist brushes
12. Exacto knives
13. abrasive paper in grades 100, 120 and 220
14. veneer
15. an old electric iron
16. putty knife
17. tack rag
18. 3/0 or 4/0 steel wool
19. artist's colors, if desired

The four most common types of veneer problems you may encounter are:
1. Bubbles or blisters where the existing veneer has raised from the surface
2. Chipped pieces usually found on the edges
3. Loose sections near the edges
4. Missing pieces or sections that are so damaged that they have to be replaced

Albert Constantine, 2050 Eastchester Road, New York City, New York, is an excellent source for veneer. Usually the minimum amount of veneer you can order is a square foot. Most of the veneers that were used during the 1920s, 1930s and 1940s ranging from the common walnut to the exotic Carpathian burl elm are still available from this company. If you buy new veneer to use in the repairing process, you will find that it sometimes tends to be wavy. Before it can be used, it should be flattened by moistening both sides and placed under weights.

Old discarded and damaged pieces of veneered furniture provide another source for veneer. Removing the veneer involves several steps. First paint remove any existing finish on the piece, and permit it to dry before proceeding. Then, put a damp cloth on the veneer near the edge and place a hot iron on the cloth. The heat and moisture will loosen the glue. Next a putty knife can be used to pry up the loosened veneer. Often several applications with the hot iron are necesary to loosen the veneer so it can be removed without damaging it. Only steam off as large a piece as you need for the repair job you are doing.

Before you begin any repairing, you must understand that a good bond can only be obtained if the old glue is removed. New glue added to old dried glue or a dirty surface will not adhere properly.

Repairing Blisters or Bubbles

1. Place a damp cloth over the blistered surface. When a hot iron is set on the cloth, moisture will be forced into the veneer and make it more flexible and less likely to split as you work with it.
2. Use a razor blade and a straight edge to slit the bubble across the center, following the grain.
3. Scrape away the old glue under the bubble with a tool such as an Exacto knife. The steaming process used in step one should have softened the glue and made it easier to remove.
4. Place fresh glue under the veneer on one side of the slit and press the veneer down with your finger forcing out the excess. Remove the surplus with a damp cloth or paper towel and wipe dry. Follow this same procedure with the other half of the bubble.
5. Put a piece of wax paper over the area. This will prevent the glue from sticking to the gluing block. Place a gluing block, slightly larger than the damaged area, on the wax paper.
6. Weight or clamp for about 12 hours.
7. Remove clamps or weights, block and wax paper.
8. Sand the repaired area until it is smooth and free from any hardened glue.
9. Use a tack rag to pick up any dirt or dust.
10. Apply a finish over the repaired area by using a varnish or a finish of your choice.
11. Use 3/0 or 4/0 steel wool to blend the repaired section to the rest of the surface when the finish is dry. Always rub with the grain pattern of the wood.

Clamping a Repaired Section in the Center of a Table

1. Place a piece of wax paper and a gluing block, slightly larger then the damaged area, on the repair.
2. Position boards such as 2 x 4s, one above and on top of the block and one below the table top. Each should extend beyond the edge of the table. Use a C clamp or bar clamp to hold these boards tightly at each end so the gluing block is under pressure.

Repairing Loose Veneer Near the Edge

1. Moisten the loose veneer with a damp cloth. When a hot iron is set on the cloth, moisture is forced into the veneer, making it more pliable and less apt to split.
2. The application of heat and water explained in step 1 will loosen the hardened glue and make it easier to remove with an Exacto knife.
3. Use the knife's edge to lift the loosened veneer and to spread glue on the surface beneath.
4. Press down on the veneer with your finger to work out the excess glue. Then wipe off the surplus with a damp cloth or paper towel.
5. Follow steps 5 through 11 as explained under **Repairing Blisters or Bubbles**.

Replacing Missing Veneer

(The most exacting part in this process is fitting the new piece of veneer into the "bed" or "grave", the depression on the surface from which the damaged veneer has been removed.)

1. Use a straight edge and single edge razor blade and cut away the damaged veneer. Cut with the grain so the ends of the "Grave" follow the flow of the grain and end in a point as in the shape of a diamond.
2. Do not use a square shaped piece of veneer for it will make the repaired area too noticeable.
3. Clean away any dirt or hardened glue. A damp cloth and hot iron, as explained under point 1 in **Repairing Blisters or Bubbles**, can be used for this purpose.
4. Make a template of the "bed" by placing a piece of paper over it and pressing the edges with your finger to form a pattern.
5. Cut out the pattern with scissors and test to see that it fits snugly into the "bed". Adjustments may have to be made until you get a perfect fit.
6. Trace this pattern onto the piece of veneer you will be using for the repair and cut the marked line with a razor and a metal straight edge.
7. Use abrasive paper, if necessary, on the edges of the repair patch until it fits snugly into its "bed".
8. Put a thin layer of glue in the "bed" and place the veneer patch over the glue.
9. Press down on the veneer with your fingers to work out the excess glue and wipe away the surplus with a damp cloth or paper towel.
10. Put a piece of wax paper and a gluing block that is larger than the repair piece over the area and clamp for about 12 hours.
11. Remove the clamp, block and wax paper and sand away any excess dried glue with abrasive paper.
12. Follow the steps 9 through 11 under **Repairing Blisters or Bubbles**.

Sometimes the chips or missing pieces are too small for veneer patches. If this is the case, a colored wood dough or putty can be used to fill the depression. After it has dried, it can be sanded with abrasive paper until it is smooth. Then it should be finished with a varnish or a finishing material of your choice. When dry, 3/0 or 4/0 steel wool can be used to blend the repaired area into the rest of the piece.

Coloring a Repaired Area

If the color of the replaced area of veneering or patching, explained under the preceding processes, does not satisfactorily match the original, you may need to use artist's oil pigments to solve the problem.

With the use of burnt umber, raw umber, burnt sienna, raw sienna, Van Dyke brown, rose pink and chrome yellow, you can mix and match almost every existing veneer color that was in use during the 1920s, 1930s and 1940s. Materials of this nature are available at artist supply stores.

1. Place a small amount of varnish or a finish of your choice on a palette-like board and to this add artists colors, stirring them in with the tip of a small brush until you achieve the color you want.
2. Apply this color on the surface with an artist brush.
3. When the finished area is dry, smooth the surface by rubbing it with the grain with either 3/0 or 4/0 steel wool.

Patent Serial Numbers and Dates Issued

Year	Patent Number	Year	Patent Number
1920	1,326,899	1936	2,026,510
1921	1,364,063	1937	2,066,309
1922	1,401,948	1938	2,101,004
1923	1,440,362	1939	2,142,080
1924	1,478,996	1940	2,185,170
1925	1,521,590	1941	2,227,418
1926	1,568,040	1942	2,268,540
1927	1,612,790	1943	2,307,007
1928	1,654,521	1944	2,338,081
1929	1,696,897	1945	2,366,154
1930	1,742,181	1946	2,391,856
1931	1,787,424	1947	2,413,675
1932	1,839,190	1948	2,433,824
1933	1,892,663	1949	2,457,797
1934	1,944,449	1950	2,492,944
1935	1,985,878		

Glossary

Apron
The portion under a chair seat, at the base of cabinets, cupboards and chests and beneath the top on tables.

Art Deco
A name developed after the Paris Exposition in 1966 that commemorated the Exposition Internationale des Arts Décoratifs et Industriels Modernes of 1925.

Art Moderne
An extreme, modernistic French decorative style that was displayed at the Exposition Internationale des Arts Décoratifs et Industriels Modernes in Paris in 1925.

Artificial Graining
The result obtained when stain or paint is applied to wooden or metal furniture to imitate the grain of a specific wood.

Bakelite
The first synthetic resin. A plastic sometimes used for furniture handles or accessories during the early 1900s.

Bevel
A slanting edge on wood or a mirror.

Bird's-eye Maple
A pattern, vaguely resembling birds' eyes, found in some maple trees.

Bleached
Woods, such as walnut or mahogany, treated to appear light in tone.

Blockfront
Front of a desk or chest composed of a concave center panel flanked by two convex panels with arches or carved shells at the top.

Blonde
Bleached woods or naturally light woods such as maple, holly, aspen, birch, avodire or prima vera.

Book Matching
Two consecutive sheets of veneer, opened like a book, glued side by side.

Book Trough
A small table with a V-shaped shelf for holding books.

Borax
The name applied to the mass produced, lower priced, poorly made, showy furniture of the 1920s and 1930s.

Breakfront
A bookcase, desk or cupboard made of three sections. The center one projects out vertically beyond the other two sections, breaking the straight line of the front.

Brocade
An embossed upholstery fabric.

Broken Pediment
A top ornament on a secretary or a bookcase that does not meet at the highest point.

Buffet Mirror
A long, low mirror usually divided into three or four parts. Also called a landscape or mantle mirror.

Burl
Mottled or speckled veneer from the diseased, hump-like growth on trees.

Butt
Decorative veneers cut from the section of the tree where the roots spread away from the trunk. Also called stump.

Butterfly Table
A petite table with two drop leaves that, when raised to a horizontal position, are supported by a swinging bracket resembling a butterfly wing.

Cabriole Leg
A leg with a double curve that bulges out at the knee, sweeps inward and flows out slightly at the ankle.

Case Piece
Box-like structures such as chests of drawers, cabinets and desks.

Cedar Chest
A cedar or cedar-lined lift-lid chest that protects garments, blankets and furs from moths.

Cellarette
A liquor cabinet.

Celluloid
A man-made substance used for drawer handles, dresser sets and novelties.

Channeled
A grooved or furrowed effect in wood. Also called ribbed.

Cheerio Cabinet
A liquor cabinet.

Chest-on-chest
A high chest that resembles one chest placed upon another. Also called highboy.

Chiffonier
A tall, narrow chest of drawers.

Chifforette

A bedroom unit with one or two drawers at the base and two doors above. Behind the doors are sliding trays for storing personal possessions.

Chifforobe

A bedroom unit with double doors. Behind the doors on one side are drawers and on the other side is a space to hang clothes.

Chinoiserie

An ornate style of decoration based on Chinese motifs. Often painted or lacquered designs are used.

Chintz

Printed glazed cotton fabric often with floral design.

Chippendale, Thomas

An English cabinetmaker (1718?-1779) whose designs were copied in the 1920s, 1930s and 1940s.

Chromium

A hard metallic chemical element used in electroplating alloy steel. Also called chrome.

Cocktail Table

A low table usually placed in front of a davenport.

Coffee Table

A low table usually placed in front of a davenport.

Commode

A washstand with an enclosed cupboard.

Console

A table with a flat side that fits against a wall.

Console Mirror

A mirror that hangs over a console table.

Copperwash

A thin coating of liquid copper applied over a tin surface.

Crotch

Lumber cut from the fork in a tree trunk or from the places where large branches join the trunk.

Cubism

Art characterized by a separation of the subject into cubes or other geometric forms.

Curio Cabinet

A tall, narrow cabinet containing a series of shelves on which trinkets and treasures are displayed.

Damask

A durable, reversible, lustrous linen or silk fabric with a figured weave.

Davenport Bed

A davenport (sofa) that can be converted into a bed.

Davenport Table

A long table that customarily was placed behind a davenport.

Decalcomania

A picture or design printed on special paper that can be transferred to glass, wood or other surfaces. Also called decal.

Depression Era

An economically depressed period characterized by unemployment, falling prices, low wages and a slackening of business activities such as the United States experienced from 1929 through the 1930s.

Dressing Table

A table with a mirror or mirrors at which a woman sat to comb her hair and apply cosmetics. Also called vanity or toilet table.

Drop Center Vanity

A dressing table with a low center flanked by higher sides that usually included drawers or doors.

Eclectic

Copying, combining and adapting designs from the past to create furniture.

End Matching

Sheets of veneer matched lengthwise (end to end).

End Table

A small table placed at the end of a sofa or next to an upholstered arm chair.

Engraving

A design cut into a surface.

Etching

A hazy design on glass made by the corrosive action of hydrofluoric acid.

Fall Front

A hinged lid on a desk that drops down to form a writing surface.

Fibrewood

A flexible, board-like material made from pressed fibres (fibers) of wood.

Flitch

A bundle of adjacent veneers.

Four-way Matching

A combination of book and end matching.

Fretwork

An ornamental border, perforated or cut in low relief.

Fumed Oak

A dark finish on oak secured through exposing furniture to ammonia vapors.

Gate-leg Table

A drop leaf table with stretcher supported legs that swing out from the base to support the leaves.

Gesso

A plaster of Paris preparation used in sculpture and bas relief.

Gilding
Applying gold leaf or a substance like gold to a surface. Also called gilting.

Golden Oak
A gold finish (probably an orange shellac) on oak.

Grain
The arrangement and direction of fibers in wood that gives it its markings or figure. In closed grain the pores are too small to be seen readily. In opened grain the pores are large enough to be seen.

Graining
The result or stain applied to imitate the grain of a specified wood.

Hepplewhite, George
An English cabinet maker (?-1786) whose designs were copied in the 1920s, 1930s and 1940s.

Hoosier Cabinet
A generic name for a kitchen cabinet with a pull-out work space, cupboard storage, drawers, flour bin, sifters and other work-saving conveniences.

Hostess Cart or Wagon
A small push-cart with shelves used for dishes, beverages or food. Also called tea cart.

Humidor
A metal-lined smoking cabinet with a provision for keeping tobacco moist and fresh.

Inlay
Designs formed by inserting woods, ivory, metal or other materials of contrasting colors into the surface or furniture.

Jacquard
All cloths with elaborate figures requiring the use of the Jacquard loom.

Knee-hole
A desk that provides leg space between rows of drawers or doors.

Lacquer
A hard, rapidly drying finish that is combined with colored enamels to emulate Oriental designs on wood or metal.

Lamination
The result of a crisscross layering process in which several thicknesses of veneer are glued at right angles to the grain of adjacent veneers to form plywood.

Lyre
A decorative motif on chair backs and table bases that resembles a lyre, a stringed instrument.

Marquetry
The decorative result of covering a surface, such as a table top, with inlays of wood, mother-of-pearl, ivory or metal into a close-fitting pattern.

Martha Washington Sewing Stand
A small sewing cabinet with central drawers and convex ends with flat hinged tops.

Medullary Rays
Rays radiating from the center of a tree across the annual rings.

Misson
Straight lined substantial, heavy furniture usually made of oak.

Mohair
Upholstery fabric made from Angora goat hair, often mixed with other fibers.

Nest of Tables
A stack of three or more tables of gradually diminishing sizes that fit one beneath the other into a compact single position. They can be used individually.

Occasional Table
Any small table, especially those used in living rooms.

Onyx
A variety of agate with alternate layers of color.

Overlay
A decorative layer of veneers or other substances applied to a surface.

Pier Cabinet
A tall, narrow cabinet containing a series of shelves on which trinkets and treasures are displayed.

Plain-Sawed
Sawing a log in parallel lines lengthwise.

Plush
A fabric with a thick, soft, deep pile (raised surface).

Ply
One layer of veneer.

Plywood
Several layers of veneer glued together at right angles to the grain of the adjacent veneers to form a strong surface.

Pollarding
The practice of malforming a tree by cutting its top branches back to the trunk where a burl-like grain develops.

Polychrome
The application of various colors on frames, furniture carvings and metal bases.

Pore
Small openings in wood through which fluids are discharged or absorbed.

Priscilla Sewing Stand
A portable sewing stand with hinged slant lids covering the two enclosed storage units.

Prohibition
The time period when the manufacture of alcoholic beverages was prohibited.

Projection Front
A top drawer that protrudes over the rest of the drawers.

Quarter-Sawed
Sawing a log into four pieces and sawing these into parallel boards across the annual growth rings to expose the medullary rays.

Radio Bench
A low, backless bench used near a radio.

Refectory Table
A long, narrow table with underleaves that pull out to extend the surface. Also called draw table.

Ribbed
A grooved or furrowed effect in wood. Also called channeled.

Rotary-Sawed
Cutting a log by rotating it against a knife to secure large sheets of veneer.

Router
A tool that cuts recessed lines on wood or metal surfaces.

Router Lines
Incised lines made in wood or metal by a router.

Serpentine Front
A front on furniture that flows in and out.

Secretary
An enclosed desk with a bookcase top.

Server
A small serving and storage unit in a dining room used with or in place of a buffet.

Sewing Cabinet
A small storage unit for sewing materials.

Slip Matching
Sliding the top sheet of veneer from a bundle (flitch) into a side-by-side alignment with the sheet directly beneath it.

Slat
A horizontal cross bar in a chair back.

Smoker
A stand that holds smoking accessories.

Spinet Desk
A 1930 copy of early 19th century stringed instruments called spinets that were often converted into shallow writing desks.

Spindle
One of a series of turned uprights in a chair back.

Splat
The central upright in a chair back.

Stretcher
The cross piece that connects chair, cabinet or table legs near the base.

Stump
Decorative veneers cut from the section of the tree where the roots spread away from the trunk. Also called butt.

Tapestry
A heavy cloth woven with decorative designs and pictures used as a wall hanging or as upholstery fabric.

Tier Table
A table with two or three circular levels graduating in size from the largest at the base to the smallest at the top.

Tilt-Top Table
A table hinged to the top of a center post so it can be tipped to a vertical position.

Tea Cart or Wagon
A small push-cart with shelves used for dishes, beverages and food. Also called hostess cart or wagon.

Telephone Set
A small table with an attached or separate seat to accommodate the telephone, the book and the talker.

Vanity
A table with a mirror or mirrors at which a woman sat to comb her hair or apply cosmetics. Also called dressing or toilet table.

Velour
A generic term for a fabric with a short pile (raised surface).

Velvet
A rich fabric of rayon, silk or nylon with a thick, soft pile.

Veneer
A thin, decorative wood that can be glued over a common base wood to ornament furniture.

Verdigris
A rust-like green coating that forms on brass, bronze or copper.

Wardrobe
A storage closet where clothes were hung. Often it had a drawer or drawers.

Waterfall
A rounded edge used on furniture tops, mainly in the 1930s and 1940s.

Wing Chair
A high back chair on which the back projected on each side in wings to shield the sitter from drafts.

Bibliography

Books

Andrist, Ralph K., Editor in charge. *The American Heritage History of the 20s & 30s.* New York: American Heritage Publishing Co., Inc., 1970.

Aronson, Joseph. *The Encyclopedia of Furniture, Third Edition.* New York: Crown Publishers, Inc., 1965.

Constantine, Albert, Jr. *Know Your Woods.* New York: Home Craftsman Publishing Corporation, 1959.

Doan, Franklyn E., Editor. *Seng Furniture Facts.* Chicago: The Seng Company, 1964.

Grotz, George. *The Furniture Doctor.* Garden City, New York: Doubleday & Company, Inc., 1962.

Hillier, Bevis. *The Style of the Century, 1900-1980.* New York: E.P. Dutton, Inc., 1983.

Kinney, Ralph Parsons. *The Complete Book of Furniture Repair and Refinishing.* New York: Charles Scribner's Sons, 1950.

Klein, Dan. *All Colour Book of Art Deco.* London: Octopus Books, 1974.

Learoyd, Stan. *The Conservation and Restoration of Antique Furniture.* New York, N.Y.: Sterling Publishing Company, Inc. 1983.

McClinton, Katharine Morrison. *Art Deco, A Guide for Collectors.* New York: Crown Publishers, Inc., 1972.

Ransom, Frank Edward. *The City Built on Wood - A History of the Furniture Industry in Grand Rapids, Michigan, 1850-1950.* Ann Arbor, Michigan: Edwards Brothers, Inc., 1955.

Stickley Brothers Company. *Adapting Quaint Furniture to American Needs.* Grand Rapids, Michigan: Stickley Brothers Company, 1925.

Swedberg, Robert W. and Harriett. *American Oak Furniture Styles and Prices, Book II.* Lombard, Illinois: Wallace-Homestead Book Company, 1984.

Winchester, Alice. *How to Know American Antiques.* New York: The New American Library, 1951.

Yates, Raymond F. and Marguerite W. *Victorian Antiques.* New York: Gramercy Publishing Company, 1949.

Bulletins and Newspapers

Fine Hardwoods/American Walnut Association. *Fine Hardwoods Selectorama.* Indianapolis: Fine Hardwoods/American Walnut Association, 1978.

Furniture Store Advertisements. *The Moline Daily Dispatch.* Moline, Illinois: December 1935; December 1937; November 1939; October 1940; April 1947; December 1948; December 1949.

Periodicals

_____. *The Furniture World and Furniture Buyer and Decorator.* Volume CXXVII, April 13, 1933 to October 5, 1933.

_____. *Homefurnishing Arts.* Volume I, Spring, 1933.

_____. *Homefurnishing Arts.* Volume I, Fall, 1933.

_____. *Homefurnishing Arts.* Volume III, Spring and Summer, 1935.

_____. *Homefurnishing Arts.* Volume III, Fall, 1935.

Catalogues

Baker Furniture Inc. *Baker Furniture Inc. Catalog*. Holland, Michigan: 1937.

Berkey & Gay. *The Berkey & Gay Style Book*. Grand Rapids, Michigan: 1929.

Century Furniture Company. *Furniture as Interpreted by the Century Furniture Company*. Grand Rapids, Michigan: 1939.

Chittenden & Eastman Company Furniture Distributors. *Catalogues*. Burlington, Iowa: 1920-1923; 1925-1929; 1930-1932; 1934-1939; 1940-1943; 1949.

Imperial Desk Company. *Imperial Desks Catalogue Number 42*. Evansville, Indiana: 1944.

Imperial Furniture Company. *Spring and Summer Catalogue*. Grand Rapids, Michigan: 1936.

Montgomery Ward & Company. *Catalogue No. 99*. Chicago: Fall and Winter, 1923-1924.

Montgomery Ward & Company. *Catalogue Number 110*. Chicago: Spring and Summer, 1929.

Montgomery Ward & Company. *Catalogue Number 118*. Chicago: Spring and Summer, 1933.

Sears, Roebuck and Company. *Catalogue No. 154*. Chicago: Spring and Summer, 1929.

Stickley Brothers Company. Quaint Furniture. *The Old House*. Grand Rapids, Michigan: Catalog No. 45.

Reference Works

Furniture Dealers' Reference Book. Chicago: Homes Bureau, 1926.

Furniture Dealers' Reference Book. Chicago: Homes Bureau, 1928-1929.

The Random House Collector's Encyclopedia - Victorian to Art Deco. New York: Random House, 1974.

The World Book Encyclopedia. Chicago: W.F. Quarrie & Company, 1936.

The World Book Encyclopedia. Chicago: Field Enterprises Educational Corporation, 1966.

Index

FURNITURE OF THE DEPRESSION ERA
PRICE GUIDE

Schroeder's Antiques Price Guide

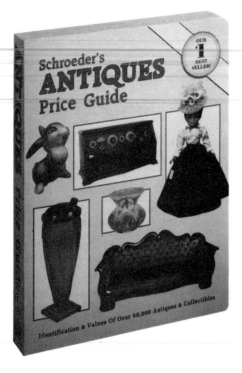

Schroeder's Antiques Price Guide has become THE household name in the antiques & collectibles field. Our team of editors works year-round with more than 200 contributors to bring you our #1 best-selling book on antiques & collectibles.

With more than 50,000 items identified & priced, Schroeder's is a must for the collector & dealer alike. If it merits the interest of today's collector, you'll find it in Schroeder's. Each subject is represented with histories and background information. In addition, hundreds of sharp original photos are used each year to illustrate not only the rare and unusual, but the everyday "fun-type" collectibles as well — not postage stamp pictures, but large close-up shots that show important details clearly.

Our editors compile a new book each year. Never do we merely change prices. Accuracy is our primary aim. Prices are gathered over the entire year previous to publication, from ads and personal contacts. Then each category is thoroughly checked to spot inconsistencies, listings that may not be entirely reflective of actual market dealings, and lines too vague to be of merit. Only the best of the lot remains for publication. You'll find Schroeder's Antiques Price Guide the one to buy for factual information and quality.

No dealer, collector or investor can afford not to own this book. It is available from your favorite bookseller or antiques dealer at the low price of $12.95. If you are unable to find this price guide in your area, it's available from Collector Books, P.O. Box 3009, Paducah, KY 42002-3009 at $12.95 plus $2.00 for postage and handling.

8½ x 11", 608 Pages   **$12.95**

COLLECTOR BOOKS
A Division of Schroeder Publishing Co., Inc.